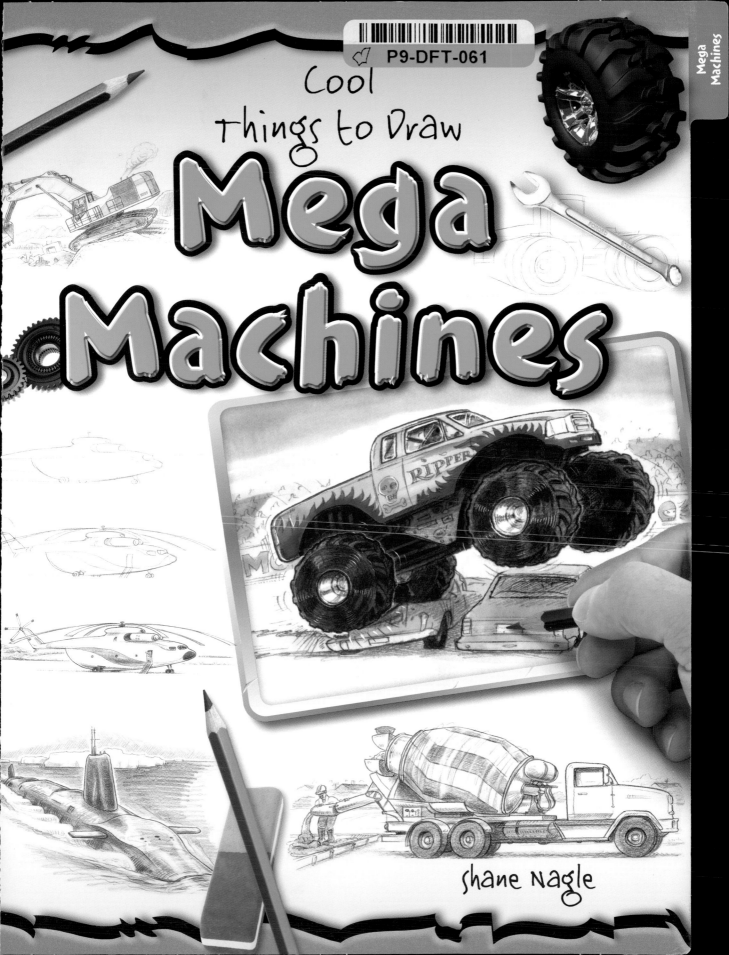

Mega Machines

Cool
things to Draw
Mega
Machines

RIPPER

shane Nagle

# Cool things to Draw
# Mega Machines

hinkler

# INTRODUCTION

The invention of machines is a perfect expression of the imagination and innovation that help our species thrive on earth. Every day, massive machines move about, lifting, moving, exploring, building and destroying. It's not all work: some are just for pure fun!

Inside these pages are some of the most incredible machines on the planet. They are amazing, not just because of what they can do, but because of how huge and powerful they are.

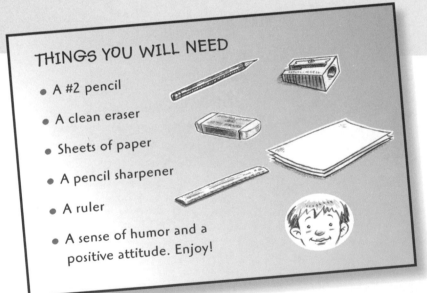

## THINGS YOU WILL NEED

- A #2 pencil
- A clean eraser
- Sheets of paper
- A pencil sharpener
- A ruler
- A sense of humor and a positive attitude. Enjoy!

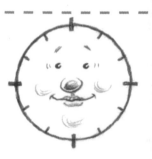

## Using Clock-face

This fun tip will help you sketch lines at different angles.

*Look at the line you want to draw.*

*Now imagine that line on a clock-face: where would it point?*

*Draw a line on your page, matching the angle on the imaginary clock-face.*

## Drawing guidelines

When drawing your mega machines, pay attention to these things:

1. Each drawing begins with basic shapes and guidelines
2. Always draw lightly at first
3. Focus on one part of the drawing at a time
4. Build texture and volume in layers
5. Experiment with different pencil techniques as you go along
6. Practice, practice, practice!

# Step-by-step drawing

Each drawing is made by following steps. Read through all the steps carefully before you begin, then follow them one at a time until your drawing is done. Don't worry if your drawing looks different to the examples; all artists find their own style and your skills will improve with practice.

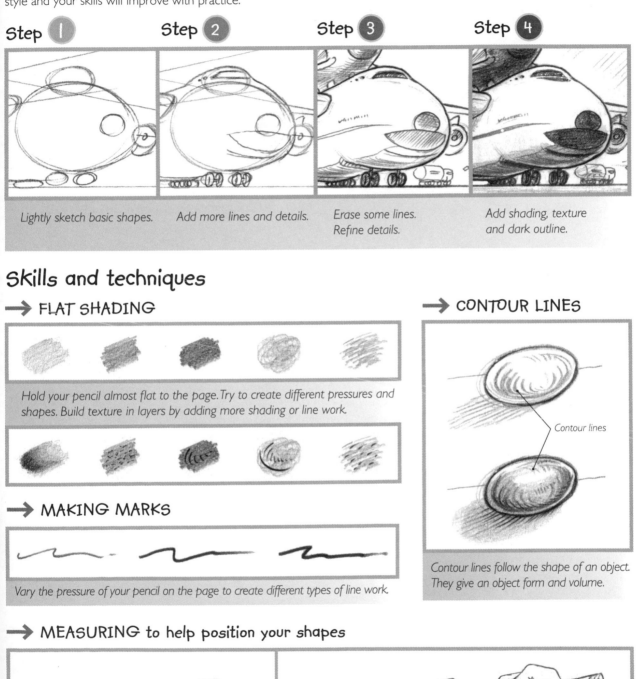

Step 1
Lightly sketch basic shapes.

Step 2
Add more lines and details.

Step 3
Erase some lines. Refine details.

Step 4
Add shading, texture and dark outline.

# Skills and techniques

## → FLAT SHADING

Hold your pencil almost flat to the page. Try to create different pressures and shapes. Build texture in layers by adding more shading or line work.

## → MAKING MARKS

Vary the pressure of your pencil on the page to create different types of line work.

## → CONTOUR LINES

Contour lines

Contour lines follow the shape of an object. They give an object form and volume.

## → MEASURING to help position your shapes

Use a pencil like a ruler, marking the distance with your thumb. Mark that length with another pencil on your paper.

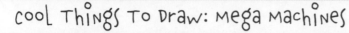

cool Things To Draw: mega machines

# CARGO PLANE

*The heavy-weight of the airplane world, the Antonov An-225 is the world's largest plane. Originally designed as an airborne tow-truck to carry a Soviet space shuttle, the Antonov is about the size of a football field and is able to lift an awesome 275 tons of cargo.*

## Before you begin

The most important element in this drawing is its use of scale. Most people know how big a space shuttle is, so to see one sitting on the back of a plane gives a good indication of the plane's size. Take your time to plot the angles and the size of the wing shapes, and always draw lightly at first.

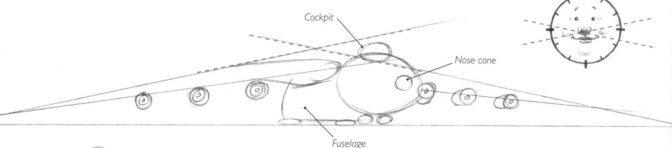

Cockpit

Nose cone

Fuselage

## Step 1

Using a ruler and a clock-face, sketch a baseline and then add three main guidelines for the wings. Use your thumb and a pencil to plot the position of the remaining shapes. Sketch a small ellipse for the *cockpit* and a large ellipse and a small circle within it for the *nose cone*. Rule the remaining guideline for the right wing. Add shapes for the six engines and the curves to the left wing. Sketch the *fuselage* shape and four ellipses for the wheels.

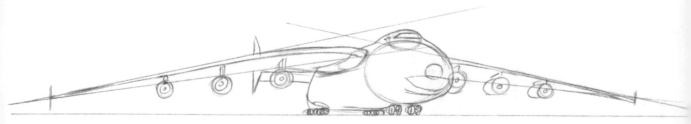

## Step 2

Sketch an outline for the top of the plane. Add window shapes and nose cone details. Draw tiny ellipses for each wheel and refine the fuselage details. Sketch additional lines on each wing, including the downward curve of the right wingtip. Add details to the engines and sketch shapes for the tail.

# Step ③

Keep drawing lightly. Using your thumb and a pencil to plot sizes, and perhaps a clock-face to check your angles, sketch the shapes for the space shuttle.

# Step ④

Erase or soften any unnecessary lines and sharpen your pencil. Refine the entire outline and add tone and details to the window and nose cone. Lightly sketch the decorative strip and add contour lines to the underside of the fuselage. Add contour lines to the inside of the engines and wheels. Refine the outline of the shuttle and add contour lines to create volume. Lightly sketch in a background and include a small figure in the foreground.

# Step ⑤

Use flat shading on all shadowed areas, including the one cast by the left wing on the fuselage. Add darker tones to the black sections of each nose cone and under the shuttle's wing and fuselage. Leave gaps along the edges of all sections to create volume. Add darker contour lines to give volume. Refine the wheel shapes with a sharp pencil and leave highlights in the center of each engine. Add clouds with a soft pencil and sketch details in the sky and background.

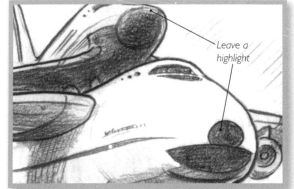

Leave a highlight

INTERESTING FACT → The six-engined An-225 can carry about 80 cars at once, and what doesn't fit inside can be carried on its back.

# CONCRETE TRUCK

*Often called cement mixers, these machines help build homes, skyscrapers and bridges by carrying wet concrete directly to a building site. Their huge drums must keep turning at all times. If they stop turning, their concrete load immediately begins to harden.*

## Before you begin

There is a lot of detail in this drawing. Notice how steps 1 and 2 set out the basic shapes of the drum, cabin and undercarriage. Take your time with these and the additional details will be easy to add.

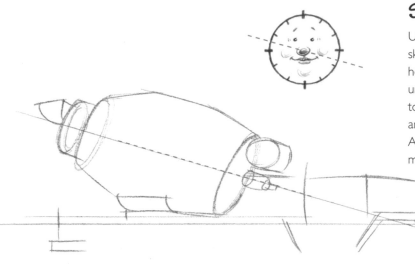

## Step 1

Using a clock-face and a ruler, lightly sketch the main angled guideline. Rule a horizontal baseline and two long lines for the undercarriage. Using a pencil and your thumb to plot their size and position, sketch ellipses and shapes for the drum and its accessories. Add lines for the front of the truck and the mudguard. Sketch in any remaining lines.

## Step 2

Still drawing lightly, add ellipses for each wheel. Sketch the remaining lines and shapes for the section below the drum and angled lines for the ground behind the truck.

## Step 3

Sketch lines for the cabin and mirror. Add details to the front of the truck, the cabin and the front wheels. Draw more lines on the undercarriage and sketch the striped pattern on the drum. Create the shapes for the chute, control panel and engine mount. Sketch mudguards and refine the wheel details. Add details to the drum's accessories.

Chute

Control panel

Engine mount

## Step 4

Erase any unnecessary lines and sharpen your pencil. Beginning with the drum and working on one section at a time, refine all details. You can even add a few more of your own. Add contour lines to the striped pattern and begin to build the shadow areas. Sketch in details on the inside of the cabin and a second baseline for the wheels (on the far side). Add tone inside and between the wheels. Add details to the chute and lights to the tail and front. Detail the bumper bar.

Contour lines help the drum appear to spin

## Step 5

Build layers of flat shading and contour lines to add volume and create shadow areas. Sketch in the human figure, the flowing concrete and a background. Refine the outlines and add small details like bolts and hinges to make the drawing appear more realistic.

Add bolts and other tiny details

INTERESTING FACT → If the concrete in a truck's drum should harden, workers have to climb in and jackhammer it out.

cool Things To Draw: mega machines

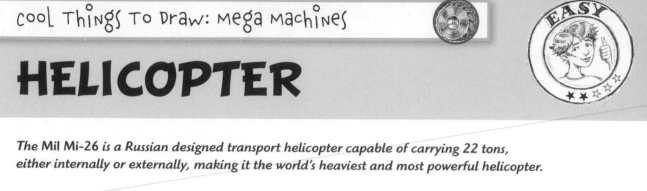

# HELICOPTER

*The Mil Mi-26 is a Russian designed transport helicopter capable of carrying 22 tons, either internally or externally, making it the world's heaviest and most powerful helicopter.*

## Before you begin

The key element of this drawing is the shape of the helicopter body itself. Notice that by adding contour lines and shading in steps 3 and 4, we give the body volume.

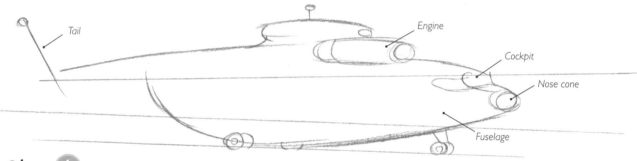

## Step ①

Lightly sketch the main three guidelines using a ruler; notice how the top one is at a slightly different angle to the bottom two. Sketch in a line for the *tail*. Add the long curved line of the *fuselage* and *nose cone*. Add curves for the *cockpit* and shapes for the upper body and *engine*. Sketch circles for the wheels and rotor anchors.

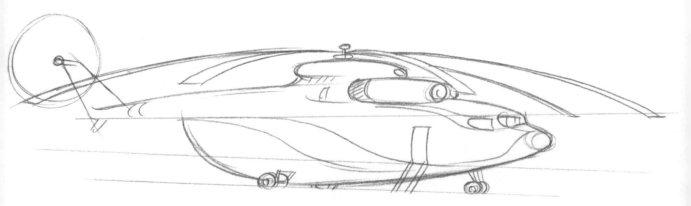

## Step ②

Keep drawing lightly. Add a circle for the tail's small propeller. Holding your pencil loosely, sketch the long curved lines for each large propeller blade. Add the S-shaped pattern to the fuselage and the small door and stairs. Refine the overall outline. Add details to the cockpit window and part of the second engine. Add any remaining line work.

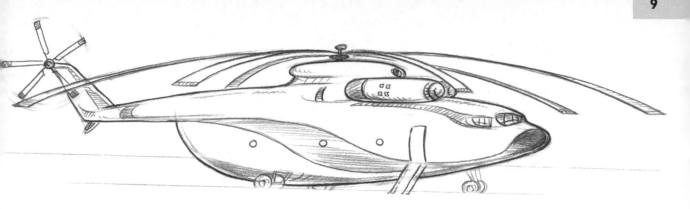

# Step ③

Erase any unnecessary lines. Refine the overall shapes and the outline with a sharp pencil, smoothing the curves as you go. Spend some time detailing the engines and cockpit. Add the small tail propeller blades. Add port holes and other fine details. Begin to give volume to the fuselage using contour lines and flat shading. Darken the nose cone.

## DRAWING TIP

Leaving highlights along edges helps give an object volume.

Shade under this blade

Leave highlights

Leave highlights

# Step ④

Refine all outlines with a sharp pencil. Darken the wheels, leaving the lower part of each broken by a line of grass. Add a long thin shadow and grassy details as your baseline. Add a second horizon line and other landscape details for the background. Add the small figure waving from the open door. Create volume by adding contour lines and flat shading, leaving highlights along each edge. Shade under two of the large propeller blades to make them appear further away.

INTERESTING FACT ➡ Originally intended for military use, the Mi-26 cargo hold can carry two armored vehicles or squeeze in nearly 150 troops.

# HYDRAULIC EXCAVATOR

*These massive excavators are ideal for digging deep trenches and preparing the ground for the foundations of buildings. They are also used in open cut mines to fill enormous tipper trucks (see pages 26–27). Their digging buckets can weigh over 3 tons, with each scoop holding 5 cubic yards of dirt and rubble.*

## Before you begin

The most complicated element of this drawing is the detail in the excavator's hydraulic arm. Take your time plotting its shape in steps 1 and 2 and the detailing will follow more easily.

## Step 1

Sketch four guidelines using a ruler and a clock-face. If you wish, plot their position using your thumb and a pencil. Drawing lightly, sketch the bucket shape and the small circles and ellipses for the arm. Create the outline of the excavator's body. Add the circles and outlines for the track-like undercarriage. Sketch in a rocky hill-top baseline.

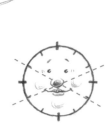

## Step 2

Lightly rule the other lines for the arm. Now rule or sketch *hydraulic unit* A. Add details for *elbow* 1 and *elbow* 2. Rule or sketch in *hydraulic unit* B. Sketch in *hydraulic unit* C and *elbow* 3. Add further details to the bucket, including the teeth. Sketch further lines for the cabin and body, including the railing. Add details to the track-type undercarriage and add a second set of tracks behind the first.

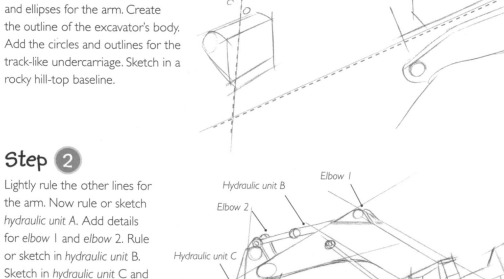

Elbow 1
Hydraulic unit B
Elbow 2
Hydraulic unit C
Elbow 3
Hydraulic unit A

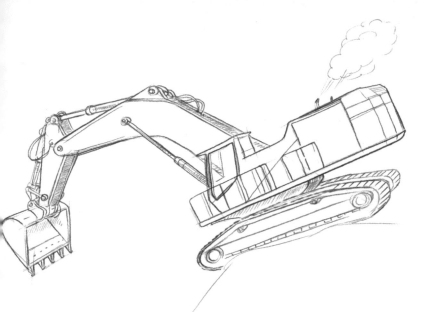

## Step ③

Erase any unnecessary lines and sharpen your pencil. Spend some time going over the line work for the three hydraulic units, the elbows and the arm itself. Draw the hoses near elbows 1 and 2 and add bolts and contour lines to the bucket. Add contour lines to the arm and to the tracks. Refine the outline of the body, cabin and railing. Add two small exhaust pipes to the top of the engine. Sketch clouds of smoke and begin to build volume with shading.

## Step ④

Refine the details using a sharp pencil. Use flat shading, cross-hatching and contour lines to create a variety of surface details. Sketch a driver and the cabin interior. Add tone to the windows and darken the undercarriage and tracks. Build a rocky baseline and a rubble-filled background. Add dirt to the bucket and give the smoke a small shadow. Add track marks in the dirt and dark shading on the ground behind the rig.

### DRAWING TIP

Press lightly when drawing objects in the background.

**INTERESTING FACT** ➔ Built for digging, not driving, this mega machine weighs nearly 94 tons but has a maximum travel speed of just 2.7mph. You could probably walk faster!

# MONSTER TRUCK

*Built for pure amusement, these monster machines evolved from the unusual sport of tractor-pulling. Eager participants began to build "raised" trucks and before long the competition was on to build the biggest. Monster trucks have 5.5 feet diameter tires and supercharged engines.*

## Before you begin

This drawing's feature is the massive tires and the detail of their tread. Take some time with the tread, using layers of flat shading and contours to help create movement, texture and volume.

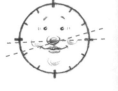

## Step 1

Using a clock-face and ruler, sketch the three ruled guidelines. Make sure the guideline for the top of the front tires is at a slightly different angle to the tire base. Sketch the main circles for the wheels and tires, plotting their size and location using your thumb and pencil. Notice that the small interior circles are off-center. Sketch in the shapes of the truck body.

## Step 2

Working on one wheel at a time, sketch in the tread pattern on each tire. Sharpen your pencil and refine the tire details, still working on one at a time. Lightly refine the outlines of the truck's body. Sketch shapes for the driver and interior and for the shock absorbers and exhaust pipes (near the rear wheel). Add axles and other shapes under the body. Draw the fourth wheel and detail the front grille.

## Step ③

Erase any unnecessary lines and soften any rough line work. With a sharp pencil, refine the overall outline, smoothing the curves as you go. Begin to add contour lines and flat shading to the tires and undercarriage. Add engine shapes and other details such as bolts and lights. Lightly sketch the outlines of the two cars beneath the monster truck.

## Step ④

Use a combination of flat shading and contour lines to build shadow areas and textures. Leave a gap around the tires to help them stand out. Add a decorative pattern to the bodywork. Leave a sheen in the wheel hubs. Lightly sketch in an audience and the stadium background. Add a shadow and further details to the crushed cars below and sketch some movement lines.

### DRAWING TIP

To make a wheel appear to spin, add radiating contour lines.

Contour lines and flat shading

Contour lines and flat shading

Leave a gap

Leave a gap

INTERESTING FACT → Monster truck rallies are public events where participants race and perform stunts in their unique machines.

**EASY**

# OIL TANKER

*These mega ships are designed to transport oil around the world. They can move nearly 2.2 billion tons of oil in a single year. Their size has grown significantly over the past forty years – the larger the ship's capacity, the less each barrel of oil costs to transport.*

## Before you begin

The main feature of this drawing is its use of perspective. Perspective is the effect that gives depth to a drawing by making long objects appear smaller the further away they are.

## Step 1

Using a clock-face and ruler, sketch the two main guidelines. Add two other ruled lines underneath (for the *hull*). Imagine that all these lines meet at a vanishing point in the distance. Sketch the curved shapes for the *bow*. Add the remaining lines and shapes for the control deck and *stern*. Holding your pencil loosely, sketch the shape of the curved horizon and the *wake trail*.

Wake trail

Stern

Bow

Hull

## Step 2

Very lightly and freely sketch the water shapes around the hull. Using your ruler and imagining the same vanishing point as in step 1, add guides for the tank lids on the large deck area. Add other fine details to the control deck, such as the smoke funnel. Begin to refine the overall outline.

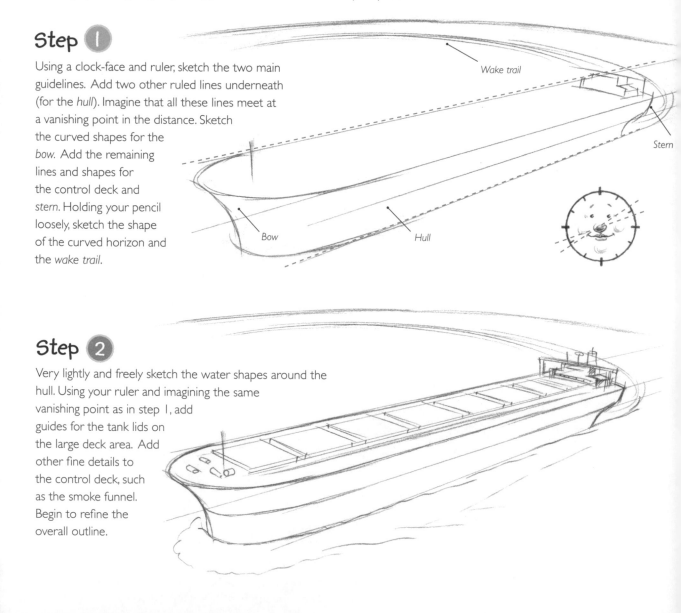

# Step ③

Erase any unnecessary lines. Pressing lightly, add contour lines to the
hull and control deck. Sharpen your pencil and refine the waterline,
wake trail and horizon. Refine the outline of the tanker's hull, bow
and stern, smoothing the curves as you go.
Use your ruler for the straight lines
if necessary.

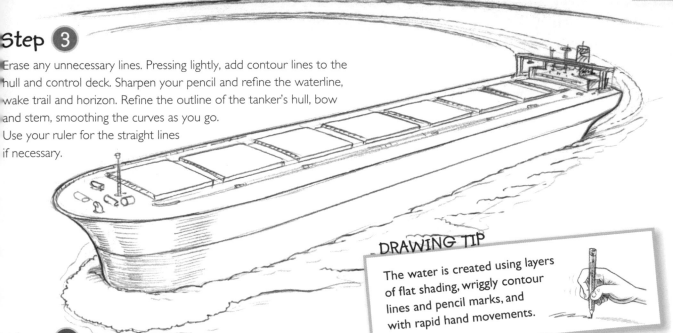

## DRAWING TIP

The water is created using layers
of flat shading, wriggly contour
lines and pencil marks, and
with rapid hand movements.

# Step ④

Lightly sketch a cloud of smoke. Use flat shading and wriggly contour lines to build the ocean. Use rapid movements of
your hand to help add texture and depth. Leave most of the water white around the base of the hull, adding just a few
soft, wriggly lines. Darken the hull with layers of flat shading and contour lines, leaving highlights to show its metallic surface.
Leave the deck mostly white but refine the tank lid outlines. Add a skyline.

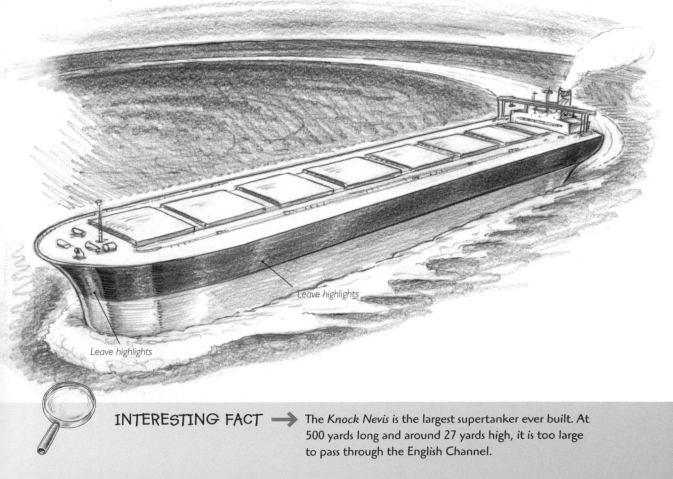

*Leave highlights*

*Leave highlights*

INTERESTING FACT ➡ The *Knock Nevis* is the largest supertanker ever built. At
500 yards long and around 27 yards high, it is too large
to pass through the English Channel.

# SUBMARINE

*Submarines dive deep below the ocean's surface. The largest of them are built for military purposes. The British Royal Navy's Vanguard class of submarine is nuclear powered, carries over 130 personnel, measures 164 yards long and weighs nearly 18 000 tons.*

## Before you begin

The main elements of this drawing are the large areas of tone (so be ready for lots of flat shading in step 4) and the use of perspective. You'll remember that perspective gives depth to a drawing by making long objects appear to be getting smaller as their distance increases.

## Step 1

Draw lightly at first. Using a clock-face and ruler, sketch the two main guidelines. Add two horizontal ruled guidelines for the *hydroplane* and the horizon. Sketch the base ellipse and other line work for the *observation tower*. Add lines for the *stern's* rudder. Sketch the two hydroplane wings. Add the remaining lines and shapes for the upper *hull*.

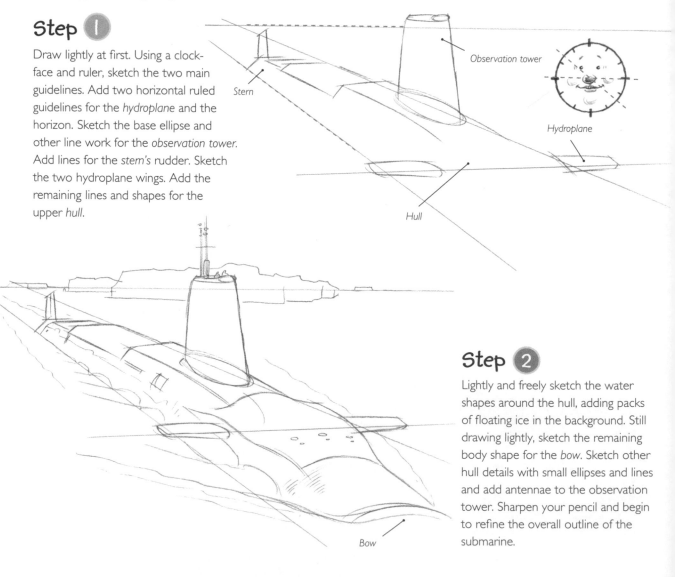

Stern

Observation tower

Hydroplane

Hull

Bow

## Step 2

Lightly and freely sketch the water shapes around the hull, adding packs of floating ice in the background. Still drawing lightly, sketch the remaining body shape for the *bow*. Sketch other hull details with small ellipses and lines and add antennae to the observation tower. Sharpen your pencil and begin to refine the overall outline of the submarine.

## Step 3

Erase or soften any unnecessary lines. Pressing lightly, add contour lines to the water over the bow and to the hull, observation tower and rudder. Sharpen your pencil and refine the wriggly waterline and wake trail. Refine the overall outline of your drawing, smoothing the curves as you go.

## Step 4

Use flat shading and wriggly contour lines to build the ocean. Use rapid hand movements to help add texture and depth. Leave most of the water white around the base of the hull, adding just a few soft, wriggly lines. Darken the hull with layers of flat shading and contour lines. Leave highlights to show the metallic surface. Add a skyline and refine the ice pack outline with a sharp pencil, making sure you don't press too heavily.

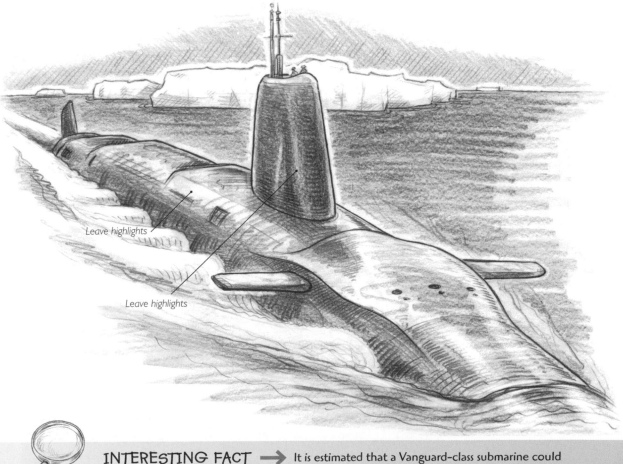

*Leave highlights*

*Leave highlights*

INTERESTING FACT ➡ It is estimated that a Vanguard-class submarine could circumnavigate the world 40 times without refueling.

# TIPPER TRUCK

*Tipper trucks come in all shapes and sizes, but they are all used to transport dirt, sand, rocks or other materials. The giant versions of these machines are specially designed for the mining industry and other major earthworks projects. This truck can carry 240 tons per load and can tip it out in just over 20 seconds.*

## Before you begin

Examine the structure of this drawing. It has three main areas: (1) the body, (2) the wheels and (3) the dirt and background. Use your ruler freely to help build and refine the body. Use lots of contour lines and scratchy marks to create the dirt.

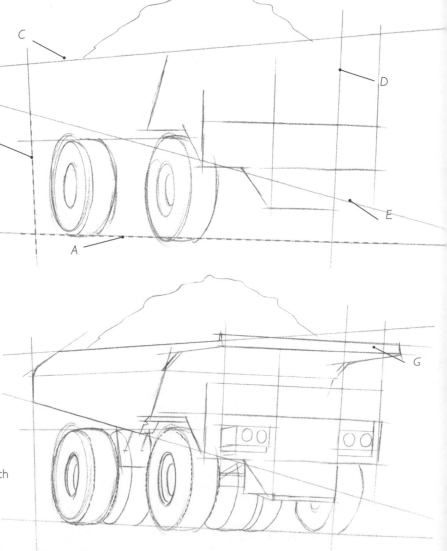

## Step 1

Using a clock-face to check the angles, rule the four main guidelines (A, B, C and D), noticing that none of these lines are parallel. Plot their location using your thumb and pencil. With a loose grip, lightly sketch all the wheel ellipses, noticing that the front wheel appears slightly larger than the rear. Rule guideline E for the bottom of the tray. Add the remaining lines for the front of the tipper. Sketch an outline for the pile of dirt.

## Step 2

Sketching lightly, add ellipses for the remaining four wheels. Begin to refine the shape and tread of the main wheels (from step 1). Lightly rule more guidelines for the tray's outline, including the overhanging front section G. Sharpen your pencil and begin to refine the tray's outline. Add details such as the railing, lights and rear mudflap.

# Step ③

Soften or erase any unnecessary lines. Sketch in a *cabin* and *tank*. Draw in three ladders, a *radiator grille* and other railings at the front. With a sharp pencil (and a ruler if necessary), refine the outlines of the tray, cabin, railings, tank, radiator and ladders. Define the wheels and tires. Darken the remaining body parts, adding details as you go. Add contour lines to the tires and details to the pile of dirt.

# Step ④

Use flat shading and contour lines to add texture and movement to the tires. Build dark layers using flat shading, pencil marks and contour lines for the dirt and undercarriage. Shade beneath the tray and roof. Add tone to the cabin, tank and windows and sketch the faint silhouette of a driver. Using a sharp pencil, further refine the drawing's outlines. Add texture to the ground and sketch in a background. Use your eraser and soft contour lines to create clouds of dust.

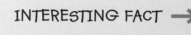

INTERESTING FACT ➡ The massive tires on this tipper are over 11 feet tall. That's about twice the height of an adult.

cool Things To Draw: mega machines

# TRACTOR

*Tractors are so named because of the high level of "traction" or grip given by their large, treaded tires. Designed to operate on loose soil and other wet or porous surfaces (like plowed fields), tractors are typically used to pull harvesters and other equipment around farms.*

## Before you begin

This drawing's main feature is the massive wheels and the detail of the tire's tread. Use layers of flat shading, contour lines and heavy line work to give your wheels detail and volume.

## Step 1

Using a clock-face and ruler, sketch guidelines A and B, noticing they are not completely parallel. Add guideline C. Rule vertical lines for the exhaust stacks and sketch a baseline for the front tires. Holding your pencil loosely, sketch the main circles for the wheels and tires, plotting their size and location using your thumb and a pencil. Notice that the interior circles are off-center. Sketch the shapes of the tractor body.

## Step 2

Sketch a rough tread pattern on the two closest tires. Lightly sketch shapes for the remaining four tires and then sharpen your pencil and begin to refine their details. Sketch shapes for the two *mudguards*, exhaust stacks, driver's seat and cabin interior, steps, front *grille* and undercarriage. Refine the line work of the tractor's body.

# Step ③

Erase any unnecessary lines and soften any rough line work. With a sharp pencil, refine the tractor body outline, smoothing the curves as you go. Refine the mudguards before working on the final tire tread, as part of the tread is hidden by them. Sketch further tread guides to the other tires before refining all tread and wheel details with a sharp pencil. Begin to add contour lines to the cabin, tires and undercarriage. Add shapes and other details, such as lights, a reflector, wheel bolts and cabin windows. Lightly sketch in a grassy ground-line under each tire.

## DRAWING TIP

Add reflections to a window using swipes of your eraser.

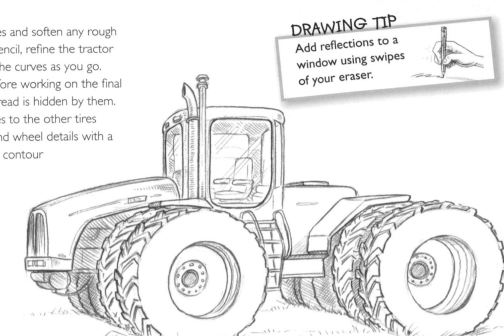

# Step ④

Use a combination of flat shading, cross-hatching and contour lines to build shadow areas and texture. Add volume to the tractor body using subtle shading, but leave shine in the wheel hubs. Add tufts of grass and use cross-hatching on the ground. Darken the engine-bay area and lightly sketch in a farm background.

Show volume using contour lines and shading

Contour lines and flat shading

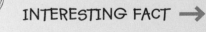
INTERESTING FACT → The most powerful modern tractors feature specially designed leather seats with variable heating and suspension systems.

MEDIUM

# BUCKET-WHEEL EXCAVATOR

*The bucket-wheel excavator (BWE) is a continuously rotating excavation machine capable of removing up to 16 000 cubic yards of material per hour. Used for mining, they are the largest earthmovers in the world. Some take five years to assemble and they can cost over $100 million.*

## Before you begin

Examine the structure of this drawing. It has four main areas: (1) the bucket-wheel, (2) the steel framework, (3) the control decks and undercarriage and (4) the background. Use your ruler freely to help build and refine the steel framework. Draw the BWE as large as possible on your page so you can add lots of details.

## Step 1

Using a clock-face, rule the four main guidelines (A, B, C and D), noticing where they intersect. Plot their position using your thumb and pencil, and add a horizon line. Rule a vertical line parallel to guideline D and a line parallel to guideline C. Sketch in the long curved line E for the excavated earth. With a loose grip, lightly sketch ellipses for the bucket-wheel. Sketch line work for the control decks and undercarriage.

*Close-up of the bucket-wheel*

## Step 2

Working on one part at a time, lightly rule more guidelines for the steel framework. Study the close-up of the bucket-wheel and lightly sketch these shapes. Add lines for the control deck and sketch the outline of the track-type undercarriage.

# Step ③

Soften or erase any
unnecessary lines.
Sketch in a tiny car and
a second bucket-wheel
excavator in the distance.
Add structural lines to the steel
framework and sketch guidelines F
for the conveyor belt sections. Refine
the detail of the bucket-wheel, leaving some
areas white for the dust clouds. Add cranes and
other tiny details to the ends of each tower and to
the far end of the excavator frame. Build tone and add
details to the control decks and the undercarriage.

F

F

Create clouds of dust

# Step ④

Use flat shading, cross-hatching and contour lines to add shadows and build volume. Keep your pencil very sharp as
you refine the steel framework, using your ruler if necessary. Refine the details of the bucket-wheel, control decks and
undercarriage and add more fine details, such as small circles to the conveyor belt and radiating contour lines to the bucket-
wheel itself. Darken the shaded areas of the excavated earth using contour lines and scratchy line work. Add the sky and
other soft details in the background. Use your eraser and soft contour lines to create clouds of dust.

INTERESTING FACT ➡ One of the largest BWEs, the Bagger 288, has 18 buckets
of 70.8 feet in diameter. These buckets are able to hold
8.6 cubic yards of dirt.

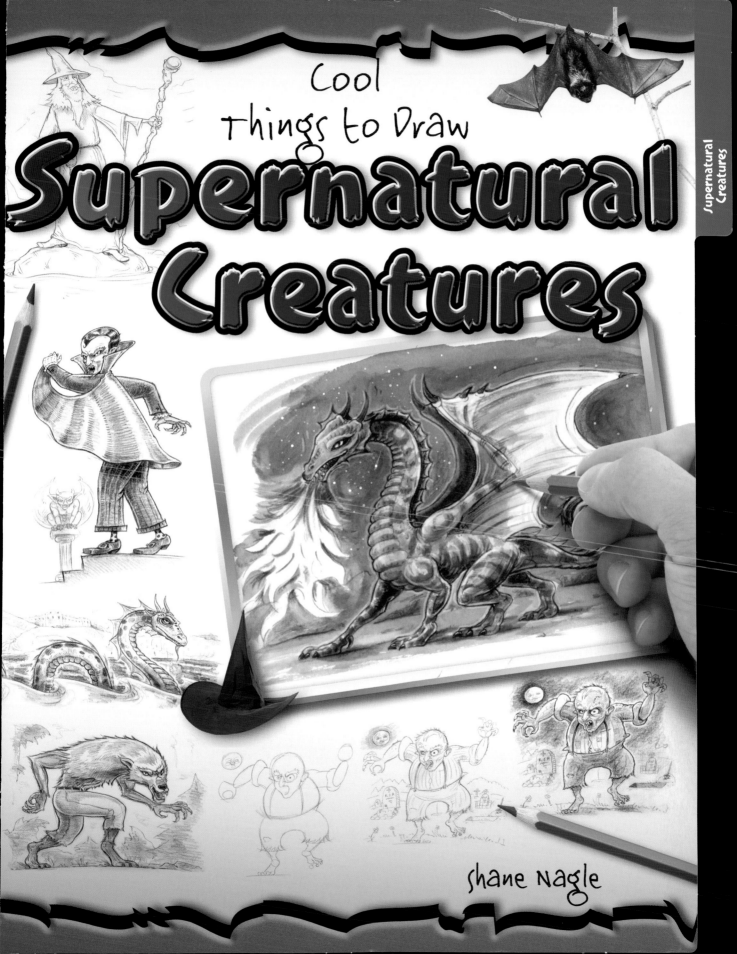

Cool
things to Draw

# Supernatural
# Creatures

Shane Nagle

# Cool Things to Draw
# Supernatural Creatures

# INTRODUCTION

*There's lots of detail in these drawings of supernatural creatures. You'll be creating claws, fangs, fur, muscles, and spears, so have your pencil sharp and ready for detail!*

*Supernatural creatures need shading to make them look scary. Experiment with different backgrounds as you become more confident. Create your own battle scenes, invent spooky eyes, and, most of all, have fun!*

## THINGS YOU WILL NEED

- A #2 pencil
- A clean eraser
- Sheets of paper
- A pencil sharpener
- A ruler
- A sense of humor and a positive attitude. Enjoy!

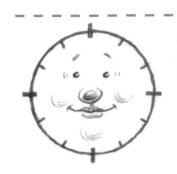

## Using the clock-face

This fun tip will help you sketch lines at different angles. *Look at the line you want to draw.*
*Now imagine that line on a clock-face: where would it point?*
*Draw a line on your page, matching the angle on the imaginary clock-face.*

## Drawing guidelines

When drawing your supernatural creatures, pay attention to these things:
1  Each drawing begins with basic shapes and guidelines
2  Always draw lightly at first
3  Focus on one part of the drawing at a time
4  Build texture and volume in layers
5  Experiment with different pencil techniques as you go along
6  Practice, practice, practice!

# Step-by-step drawing

Each drawing is made by following steps. Read through all the steps carefully before you begin, then follow them one at a time until your drawing is done. Don't worry if your drawing looks different to the examples; all artists find their own style and your skills will improve with practice.

**Step 1**  **Step 2**  **Step 3**  **Step 4**

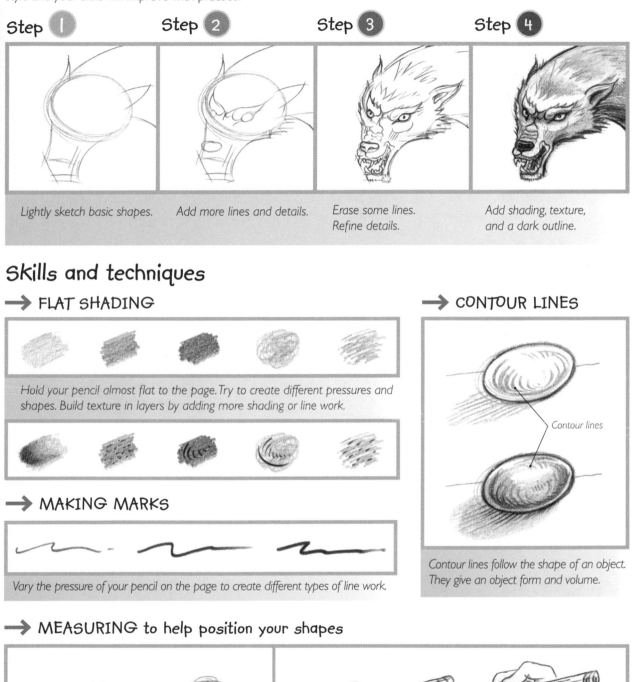

*Lightly sketch basic shapes.*  *Add more lines and details.*  *Erase some lines. Refine details.*  *Add shading, texture, and a dark outline.*

# Skills and techniques

## → FLAT SHADING

*Hold your pencil almost flat to the page. Try to create different pressures and shapes. Build texture in layers by adding more shading or line work.*

## → MAKING MARKS

*Vary the pressure of your pencil on the page to create different types of line work.*

## → CONTOUR LINES

Contour lines

*Contour lines follow the shape of an object. They give an object form and volume.*

## → MEASURING to help position your shapes

*Use a pencil like a ruler, marking the distance with your thumb. Mark that length with another pencil on your paper.*

# CENTAUR

*Centaurs featured in the mythology of ancient Greece. This half-man, half-horse creature was usually depicted as wild and unpredictable, but there were some centaurs who were wise teachers. It is thought the idea of the centaur came from cultures without access to horses seeing riders mounted on horses and mistaking them for a single creature.*

## Before you begin

The shape of the centaur is created by lots of ellipses and a bit of shading. Use a ruler and the clock-face to help measure angles, but don't get too fussy. Mistakes are allowed, and the best drawing tip is to practice.

## Step

Always draw lightly at first. Draw two large angled ellipses, holding your pencil gently and moving your arm to smoothly make the shapes. Use the clock-face to help draw the ruled guidelines at the correct angles. Notice that the vertical line leans slightly to the right. Add a curved baseline and a small circle for the hand holding the bow.

## Step 2

Keeping a gentle grip and a loose arm, lightly sketch the shapes of the body. Imagine you are building the centaur's muscles. Sketch circles and ellipses for the centaur's arm muscles, head, and leg joints. Add a c-shaped curve for the bow and curved lines for the back and legs.

## Step 3

Keep sketching lightly, building the legs, tail, face, hands, and body. Add details to the bow and the chest. Drawing all but one foot off the ground creates a sense of movement and tension in the drawing.

## Step 4

Erase any unnecessary lines, such as the vertical guideline. Using a sharp pencil, create a strong outline. Add wisps of hair to the head and a look of concentration to the face. Begin to define the centaur, adding contour lines and shading to the body.

## Step 5

Using the side of your pencil, add shading to the hair, tail, and hooves and to any area that is underneath another body part. Build up the shapes and the volume of the body using contour lines and shading. Lightly draw in mountains on the horizon, some grass, and a cloud in the sky.

INTERESTING FACT 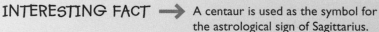 A centaur is used as the symbol for the astrological sign of Sagittarius.

# CYCLOPS

*In Greek mythology, a Cyclops was a lawless giant with one central eye in its forehead. The word "Cyclops" means "round eye." Odysseus (also known as Ulysses) defeated a Cyclops after the battle of Troy. The Cyclopes were known as excellent builders and weapon-makers, and it is thought they made Zeus's thunderbolt (the king of the gods), Poseidon's trident (the sea god) and Hades' helmet of invisibility (the god of the underworld).*

## Before you begin

This drawing is easier than it looks. Use a ruler and the clock-face to sketch the long guidelines, and mark out the distances using your thumb and a pencil. Don't worry about making mistakes or smudging the page: the Cyclops hardly ever washed! A curved baseline will help this creature look enormous.

## Step

Drawing lightly, start with a large ellipse, then add the ruled guidelines. Add a circle for the head and shapes for the upper arm and hand. Sketch guidelines for the shirt and the bottom of the Cyclops's garment and add a curved baseline.

## Step

Still drawing lightly and fairly quickly, add the other ellipses and lines that make up the arms, body, and legs. Add detailed shapes to the head and face. Draw a belt around the belly and begin to show the torn clothes using broken lines. Sketch a shape for a club and add the manacle around the ankle.

# Step ③

Erase any unnecessary lines. Add some circles for the flying rocks, a low horizon of trees, and a castle. Using a sharp pencil, define the body, face, feet, and clothes with a strong outline. Make your line-work more interesting by varying the pressure of your pencil. Use a jagged, broken line for the ripped edge of the shirt. Draw the fingers, using your own hands as a guide. Define the Cyclops's bumpy club.

## DRAWING TIP

To create flat-shading, hold your pencil almost flat to the paper. Move it in circles, with a back-and-forth action, or scribble with it to create a more interesting texture.

# Step ④

Add texture to the shirt and club, sketching stitches, rips, patches, lumps, dirt, and shadows. Build up the volume of body parts with layers of flat-shading, contour lines, and a variety of pencil marks. Add hair to the chest, beard, and legs, and some movement lines to the rocks. Create shading on the belt, club, and around the eye, and use a heavy, sharp pencil line for the face and body details.

*Add details to the castle in the background*

INTERESTING FACT → The idea of the Cyclops may have been inspired by the ancient Greeks' discovery of even older dwarf elephant skulls on the islands of Crete and Sicily. The skull's trunk-hole would have seemed a perfect location for a large eye.

# DRAGON

*Dragons have appeared in myths, legends, and folktales from around the world for thousands of years. Some dragons are fierce, while others are gentle and protective. Most dragons have wings but some don't need wings to fly. In Asian mythology, dragons are regarded as symbols of good luck and health.*

## Before you begin

Use lots of shading to give this drawing texture and volume. Experiment with a variety of pencil marks, line-work, and shading styles. You will find a way of drawing that suits you if you keep experimenting and practicing.

## Step 1

Draw smoothly and lightly at first. Use a pencil and your thumb to measure distances, and your ruler to sketch the two baselines. Sketch two angled ellipses, using the clock-face to help with the angles, if necessary. Add a shape for the head and a circle for the swirl of the tail. Sketch a small circle in one ellipse for the leg joint and lines for the wings.

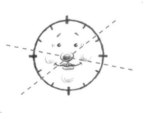

## Step 2

Focus on one body part at a time. Add s-shaped lines for the neck, then sketch the back and tail. Add the wings and legs and sketch in the details for the head. Draw two feet on each baseline to give the drawing a sense of perspective.

## Step ③

Erase any unnecessary lines. Using a light pencil, add flames coming out of the mouth. Lightly sketch the details of the neck. Sharpen your pencil and go over the outline and the major details with a heavy line, varying the pressure and angle of your pencil to make your line-work more interesting. Use contour lines and flat-shading to build volume. Add details to the wings and spikes to the tail. Define the head and facial features.

## Step ④

Use flat-shading in the background behind the flames to make them stand out. Shade the wings, underbelly, tail, legs, and neck to create depth and texture. Add contour lines and a variety of pencil-marks to create the skin texture. Define the head using a combination of sharp, dark lines and soft gray ones.

### DRAWING TIP

To give an object volume, shade close to the outline, but leave a small gap along the edge. This creates a highlight, which stops a drawing looking flat.

*Gap creates highlight*

INTERESTING FACT → Some psychologists say that if a person dreams of a dragon, it symbolizes that they are gaining self-confidence and wholeness in their life.

# GARGOYLE

*A gargoyle is a sculpture of a fantastic creature that is often mounted on cathedrals, public buildings, and old homes. Gargoyles have been found on buildings since ancient times. Traditionally, they served two functions. Firstly, they served as a water spout to drain rainwater from the roof. Secondly, the gargoyle's ugly features were thought to scare away evil spirits and protect all who entered the building.*

## Before you begin

This drawing is made from simple, basic shapes, with the only real detail required in the face, hands, and feet. Practice this one to gain your drawing confidence. Hold your pencil gently and keep your arm loose as you sketch the initial ellipses and guidelines. The bigger the ellipse, the looser your arm needs to be to draw it easily.

## Step

Sketch a curved baseline and add a half-circle cup shape curving over it. Add a large ellipse, overlapping it over the cup shape. Draw a smaller ellipse inside the large one, ensuring that it touches the top edge of the larger one. Add guidelines for the arms.

## Step

Drawing lightly, sketch an ellipse for the head. Add shapes for the ears, horns, and chin. Then, using the straight lines as a guide, sketch four ellipses for each arm, then the two for each leg. Add another curved line just above the base.

## Step ③

Erase any unnecessary lines. With a soft pencil, add details to the hands and feet. Refine the arms and legs, adding soft lines for the stomach muscles. Use soft lines for the eyes, nose, and mouth, then add more for wrinkles and cheeks. With a sharp pencil, refine the outline of the head and horns. Add contour lines to show the shape of the base and wings. Define the toes and fingers, and add teeth to the mouth.

**DRAWING TIP**

To give shadow areas texture and detail, use a variety of overlapping lines.

Use soft lines to define the features of the face

Begin to add darker lines

Cross hatching and shadow texture

## Step ④

Erase any more unnecessary lines before sharpening your pencil again. Using a heavy, sharp line, refine the outlines. Give the shadow areas depth and the body-parts volume by building layers of flat-shading and contour lines. Imagine the sun is shining down, casting shadows and leaving highlights.

**INTERESTING FACT** → In the past, people became superstitious about gargoyles, after some buildings made without them collapsed for no obvious reason.

# PHOENIX

*The phoenix is a bird found in the mythology of many cultures. It had a beautiful voice and feathers of gold and red. The phoenix lived for 500 years. When it was near death, it would build a nest of herbs and twigs, light it, and throw itself into the fire. A new phoenix would be born from the ashes.*

## Before you begin

This drawing is made up of lots of flowing lines to create the feathers and flames. To make smooth, flowing lines, keep your wrist and arm moving as you draw. Look carefully at the shapes of the wing lines. Imagine each line is a road that you are driving your pencil along. Notice how the dark background makes the phoenix look like it is full of light.

## Step ① 

Lightly draw an ellipse for the chest, using the clock-face to place it at the correct angle. Add a circle for the head and lines for the tail and wings. Use your thumb and pencil to measure distances; for example, from the shoulder to the wing-tip. Sketch a baseline and a thin ellipse under the body.

## Step ②

Sketch the features of the head and beak. Define the wings and add the heart shape on the chest. Draw the tail and the flames of the fire. Most of the lines needed in this drawing should flow like water, so keep your wrist and arm loose. You don't need to match the lines exactly; just try making them flow smoothly.

# Step ③

Erase any unnecessary lines, including the guidelines between the wing feathers, if possible. With a sharp pencil, darken and define some of the feathers, the head, and the main body outline. Add some softly drawn feathers to the wings. Add rock shapes to the fire and more detail to the wings and flames. Shade around the eye. Add contour lines to the body to build volume.

## DRAWING TIP

Shading around the eye and under the eyebrow makes the eye look realistic.

_Leave gaps so the phoenix appears to glow_

# Step ④

Use flat shading to create a strong night sky, a dark horizon, and shadows spreading out around the rocks. Keep most of the line-work inside the wings and fire soft or medium. Use dark line-work mainly in the shadow areas, leaving highlights along the edge of the rocks.

**INTERESTING FACT** ➡ The phoenix symbolizes that new things can be born from the ashes of old things.

# SEA SERPENT

Sea serpents have been part of world mythology for thousands of years. People have reported sightings of sea serpents but they have never been proven to exist. Sea serpents are said to range in length from 33–230 feet (10–70 meters) and have a horse-like head and fins down their back. It is thought they move in an up-and-down motion.

## Before you begin

Although the basic shapes of this drawing are simple, the final shaded drawing looks pretty challenging. If you wish, complete your drawing at step 3, or only do a small amount of shading at step 4.

## Step 1

Drawing lightly, create the waves, keeping your wrist and arm loose as you sketch. Draw the head and snout using the clock-face as a guide. Sketch the curves of the snake-like body.

## Step 2

Still drawing lightly, sketch in the choppy ocean in the background and a shoreline. Add details to the head, fins, and body.

## Step 3

Erase any unnecessary lines. With a soft pencil, add detail to the background. Create contour lines in the shadowed areas of the waves and body. Refine the outlines with a sharp pencil, focusing on one part at a time. Define the features of the head and body and lightly sketch in shapes on the body.

*Use a variety of shading and pencil marks to build detail*

## Step 4

Sketch a simple castle and some trees on the shore. Use flat-shading to add tone to the ocean and to add texture and volume to the body. Make the body parts near the waves quite dark. Add some dark line definition with a sharp pencil to give the drawing strength. Shade around the teeth to make them seem whiter. Add some drops of water to show movement.

**INTERESTING FACT** → Viking mythology featured a sea serpent called Jörmungandr. It was so long that it circled the whole world.

# VAMPIRE

*A vampire is a reanimated human who rises from the grave and sucks the blood of the living. Vampire myths go back thousands of years and occur in most world cultures. Vampires have no reflection in a mirror, deathly pale complexions, and the ability to turn into bats. They can be killed by a wooden stake through the heart, holy water, or sunlight.*

## Before you begin

If you draw the vampire fairly large, you can create lots of detail in the face. This vampire has a lot of shading (because vampires prefer to wear black), so be prepared to spend some time using flat-shading and creating lots of contour lines.

## Step

Drawing lightly, sketch an angled ellipse for the head, using the clock-face as a guide. Add lines for the collar and the raised arm. Focusing on one part at a time, sketch lines for the back and legs and for a baseline.

## Step

Keep drawing lightly. Draw a baseline under the figure and some stairs. Add the hairline and the details of the face. Sketch the raised hand. Add loose curves for the cloak and some contour lines where it falls on the back. Sketch the remaining arm and hand shapes. Add the ankles and shoes and a softly drawn gargoyle on a podium.

*Erase part of the ellipse to make room for face details*

## Step 3

With a soft pencil, sketch the details of the gargoyle and add contour lines to the vampire's body parts. Refine the outlines with a sharp pencil. Focus on the details of the head: pointy teeth and scary eyes are essential. Add the spots on the socks and the stripes on the trousers. Add frilly cuffs to the shirt and long, sharp finger-nails.

*Leave highlights for a greasy hair look*

*Shading and dark lines help to add expression to face*

## Step 4

Begin shading, building the shadow areas in layers. Keep your pencil sharp to help with line-work. Press heavily for shadow areas. Leave white sections to add highlights on the cloak and pants. Make the mouth dark to highlight the teeth. Use contour lines on the shoes.

**INTERESTING FACT** → Count Dracula is a fictional character, but he is thought to be based on a real cruel and blood-thirsty prince from Transylvania in the 1400s, called Vlad Drakul III. He was also known as Vlad the Impaler.

# WEREWOLF

*Werewolves are shape-shifters — humans who have the ability to turn into wolves. Stories of werewolves tell that some people become a werewolf through sorcery or a curse. These are alpha werewolves. Others became werewolves after being bitten by an alpha and from then on carry the alpha's bad blood. They are called beta werewolves. Both should be avoided on a dark night!*

## Before you begin

This drawing uses a lot of shading, so take your time with it. The shaggy fur looks complicated but if you follow the steps and focus on one thing at a time, you'll find that it is a lot easier than it looks. Once you've mastered the drawing, try creating your own backgrounds, such as a forest, volcano, or city street.

## Step

Draw lightly, sketch an ellipse for the head. Add the snout and the ears. Draw the shape of the upper body using line-work. Focusing on one part at a time, sketch the circular shapes for the thighs and lower legs. Add the feet, ankles, and a baseline under the body.

## Step

Add shapes for the eyes, whiskers, and nose to the head. Build each arm, using circular shapes to show where the muscles will be. Start to define the shape of the trousers, feet, and claws using line-work.

## Step ③

Erase any unnecessary lines. Start lightly sketching in the forest shapes in the background. With a sharp pencil, define the werewolf's features, one part at a time. Start with the head, then work on the body, clothes, and fur. Add clawed fingers and hairy legs. Add contour lines to the clothing and body.

## Step ④

Build shadow areas in layers using a variety of line-work. Keep your pencil sharp for the darker lines. Press heavily for the deep shadow areas and lightly when adding details to the fur. Highlight the teeth by making the mouth dark.

INTERESTING FACT ➔ Some werewolves can change shape at will, but most only change when there is a full moon.

# WIZARD

*Wizards are masters of magic and can either be good or bad in nature. Their powers vary according to their training and skills, but every wizard has a gift unique to them. Wizards are normally quite old, because it can take a lifetime to learn to become one. They are also cunning, intelligent, creative, and driven by a strong desire to improve their wizard powers.*

## Before you begin

This drawing uses a number of straight and slightly curved guidelines. The shaded background helps give the drawing atmosphere, but you can draw a different background if you wish.

## Step 1

Draw lightly, sketch the guideline for the wizard's staff. Add the main body lines and the lines for the arms. Sketch the shape of the pointed hat and its brim. Draw rough outlines for the rock on which the wizard is standing, the water around it, and the waterline.

## Step 2

Sketch a knotted, wooden shape around the guideline for the staff and add the wizard's hand holding it. Add an ellipse for the head and outlines for the hair and beard. Sketch shapes for the boots. Build the shapes of the hat and clothes, and add a belt and pouch. Add some ripples in the water around the rock.

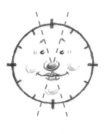

## Step ③

Erase any unnecessary lines. Sketch in the details of the background. With a sharp pencil, start refining the details of the drawing. Add the facial features to the head and define the hair and beard. Create the details of the hat and robe, such as the creases and folds. Define the staff and add contour lines to the clothing and the rock.

## Step ④

Use a variety of line-work and flat-shading to create texture and volume, building it up in layers. Soft flat-shading to the face will help make the beard look white. Keep your pencil sharp and press firmly when marking outlines. Define the background and shade the sky, water, and rock. Use line-work around the top of the staff to make it seem like the wizard is about to cast his spell!

**INTERESTING FACT** → Wizards often forget the names of their close friends because they have so many spells to remember!

# ZOMBIE

*Zombies are dead people brought back to life by magic, a curse, or other means. They are usually portrayed as mindless creatures, lacking intelligence, and with little or no memory of who they used to be. They cannot speak and tend to walk into walls. To die, a zombie must be shot, decapitated, and their brain destroyed.*

## Before you begin

The dark night sky and the full moon in this drawing give it a spooky atmosphere. This is created by using lots of flat-shading and dark shadows. Leave any smudges on the page for this drawing.

## Step

Drawing lightly, sketch an ellipse for the head. Add the body and leg shapes and a small baseline below the figure. Sketch shapes for the eyes inside the head ellipse and the chin just below it.

## Step

Erase some of the head ellipse to make room for the facial features. Sketch in the eyes, nose, mouth, ears, and eyebrows. Draw the shapes and lines for the arms and sleeves. Add lines for the braces, and shapes for the legs and feet. Don't forget the torn pants and the moon.

## Step ③

Erase any unnecessary lines. Lightly sketch the graveyard in the background and shade around the moon. Using a soft pencil, sketch the details of the shirt, pants, and fingers. Add hair and the details of the mouth and facial features. With a sharp pencil, define the outline and darken the eyes. Give him hairy arms and legs.

*Leave a gap around the zombie*

## Step ④

Build all the different textures in layers, using a variety of pencil marks. Use a very sharp pencil for the really dark outlines. Leave white highlights for where the moon is hitting the zombie. Shade the night sky and background, and the zombie's arms and clothes. Add some more tufts of hair and sketch some scars on the face. Shade the ground underneath the zombie for its shadow.

**INTERESTING FACT** → Zombies hunger for human flesh, with some preferring to eat the brains!

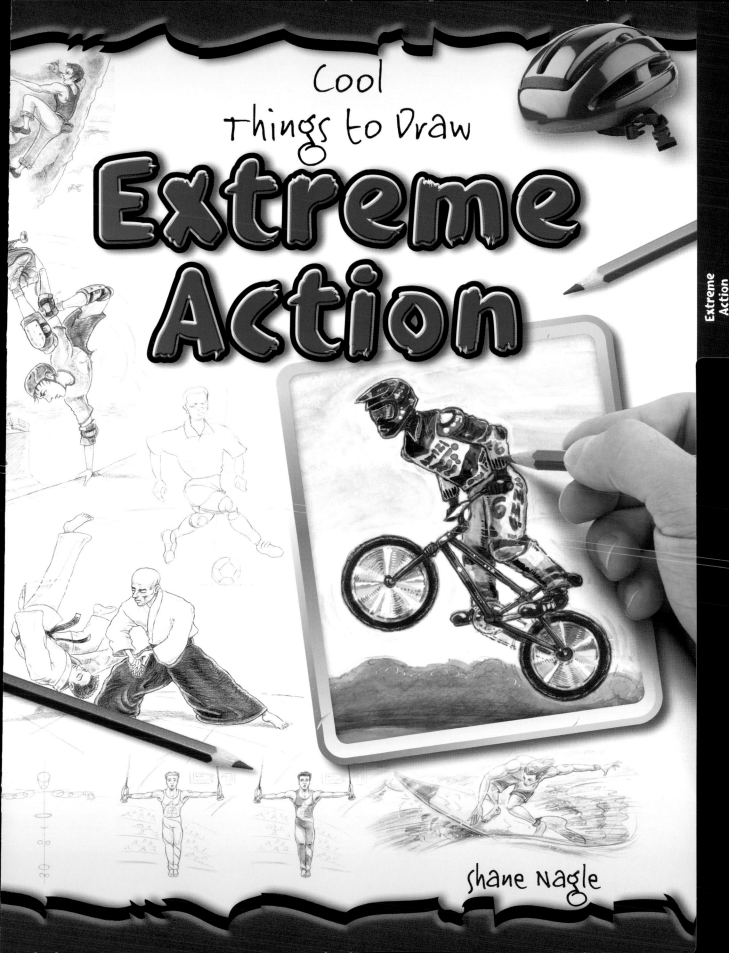

# Cool Things to Draw
# Extreme Action

Shane Nagle

# Cool Things to Draw

# Extreme Action

# INTRODUCTION

All around us people are in action: walking, running, playing games. But for some people, nothing less than heart–pumping action will do, practicing extreme activities that require skill, fitness and courage.

Learn how to draw people doing amazing things, and perhaps even be inspired to try one of them for yourself!

## THINGS YOU WILL NEED

- A #2 pencil
- A clean eraser
- Sheets of paper
- A pencil sharpener
- A ruler
- A sense of humor and a positive attitude. Enjoy!

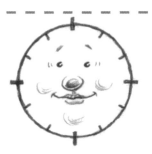

## Using Clock–face

This fun tip will help you sketch lines at different angles.

Look at the line you want to draw.

Now imagine that line on a clock-face: where would it point?

Draw a line on your page, matching the angle on the imaginary clock-face.

## Drawing guidelines

When drawing your extreme action figures, pay attention to these things:

1 Each drawing begins with basic shapes and simple lines
2 Always draw lightly at first
3 Focus on one part of the drawing at a time
4 Build texture and volume in layers
5 Experiment with different pencil techniques as you go
6 Practice, practice, practice!

# Step-by-step drawing

Each drawing is made by following steps. Read through all the steps carefully before you begin, then follow them one at a time until your drawing is done. Don't worry if your drawing looks different to the examples; all artists find their own style and your skills will improve with practice.

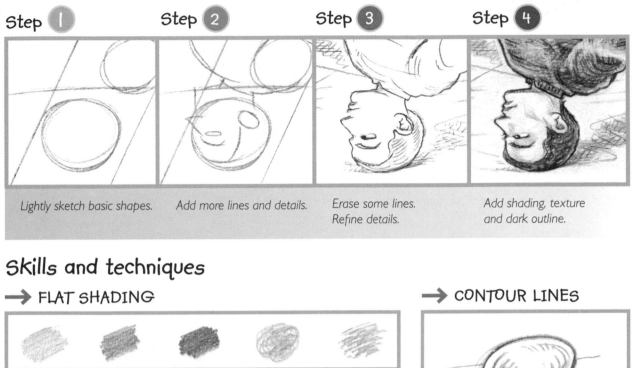

| Step 1 | Step 2 | Step 3 | Step 4 |
|---|---|---|---|
| *Lightly sketch basic shapes.* | *Add more lines and details.* | *Erase some lines. Refine details.* | *Add shading, texture and dark outline.* |

# Skills and techniques

## → FLAT SHADING

*Hold your pencil almost flat to the page. Try to create different pressures and shapes. Build texture in layers by adding more shading or line work.*

## → CONTOUR LINES

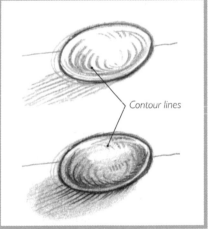

*Contour lines*

*Contour lines follow the shape of an object. They give an object form and volume.*

## → MAKING MARKS

*Vary the pressure of your pencil on the page to create different types of line work.*

## → MEASURING to help position your shapes

*Use a pencil like a ruler, marking the distance with your thumb. Mark that length with another pencil on your paper.*

cool Things To draw: Extreme Action

# AIKIDO

*Developed in Japan in the 1930s, "Aikido" means "the way of harmonizing (with) life energy". Its founder, Morihei Ueshiba, believed in blending with the energy of an attacker rather than directly opposing the attack, then redirecting that energy without causing harm.*

## Before you begin

The most important elements of this drawing are the strong angles. Notice the use of long guidelines in an A-shape in steps 1 and 2 and spend time plotting them. The angle and position of each leg and arm will help give the drawing its dynamic movement.

## Step 1

Using a ruler and a clock-face, sketch the three main guidelines. These lines are used to position all remaining shapes. Using your thumb and a pencil to measure their position, draw the two head ellipses and the three feet shapes. Add other structural lines for the standing figure's head, shoulder and arm. Sketch a long curved line from his chin down towards the floor. Sketch the remaining lines for the upside-down figure's torso and leg.

## Step 2

Work on the standing figure first. Sketch lines for the face. Add curved lines for the neck and the V-shape of the robe. Sketch the trousers, starting with the cuffs. Add lines for the bent leg. Lightly sketch the inner arm, observing its position and angle. Observe the details of the hands and then have a go at them. Sketch lines for the other figure's face and hair. Sketch the V-shape of the neck and robe and add lines for the straight arm and hand. Sketch the bent leg and foot and add a baseline.

## Step ③

Erase or soften any unnecessary lines. Replace the straight lines of the trouser-legs with wavy lines to resemble fabric in motion. Add flowing, wriggly lines to the clothes of both figures and details to their hands and feet. Refine the drawing with a sharp pencil, but don't press too heavily. Darken the heads and the facial features. With a soft pencil, add contour lines, fold lines in the fabric, hair details and movement lines. Sketch soft lines on the floor.

## Step ④

Work on the dark trousers first. Use flat shading and contour lines to build the tone. Leave highlights of lighter gray around the edges and in the fold lines. Using a sharp pencil, create strong outlines for the entire drawing, leaving gaps on the straight leg of the upside-down figure to help show the hand movement. Spend time detailing the heads, hands and feet. Add contour lines and some flat shading to the white areas of the drawing. Use cross-hatching and flat shading for the shadow on the floor.

INTERESTING FACT ➔ Some Aikido techniques involve throwing an attacker to the floor, then giving them a short massage in order to calm their anger.

# BICYCLE MOTOCROSS

EASY
★★☆☆☆

*BMX (Bicycle Motocross) began in California in the 1970s when teenagers imitated their motorcross heroes by riding bicycles offroad. This popular sport includes racing over jumps and around obstacles on specially built dirt tracks, as well as performing freestyle tricks.*

## Before you begin

Notice how the wheels appear to be turning and how far forward the figure is leaning over the handlebars. Use a ruler on this drawing, especially to help with the straight lines of the bike.

## Step 1

Using a clock-face and a ruler, sketch the angled guideline that joins the two wheel circles. Using your thumb and a pencil to plot their size and distance from each other, lightly sketch the circles for each wheel. Rule the other three angled guidelines, checking distances with your thumb and a pencil. Sketch the main ellipse for the helmet. Add the other ellipses for the helmet and lightly sketch the remaining ellipses.

## Step 2

Still drawing lightly, add lines to the helmet. Quickly sketch in the handlebars. Sketch the outline of the torso and both arms. Create the neck lines, chest and wrist shapes. Draw both legs, checking their angles against the existing guidelines. Using your ruler, add light lines for the bike frame. Sketch in shoes and other circles to the wheels.

## Step ③

Erase any unnecessary lines, especially on the helmet. Refine the drawing with some slightly darker line work. Sketch a bumpy line for the tread on the tires and a wriggly line for the jacket and trousers. Use your ruler and a sharp pencil to darken the lines of the bike frame. Add contour lines and other details to the frame. Sketch the seat and the bike chain. Add contour lines to the wheels where the spokes are spinning. Begin to build texture in the tires using contour lines. With a soft pencil, add contour lines and design features to the jacket and trousers. Sketch a baseline, a treeline and a shadow on the ground.

*Contour lines help the wheels appear to spin*

*Leave a gap*

### DRAWING TIP

Leave gaps around objects to help them stand out, and press lighter on areas to make them seem further away.

## Step ④

Build volume on the bike and body with flat shading, contour lines, cross-hatching and pencil marks. Leave highlights along the edges. Shade the straight leg and give it a softer outline so it appears to be further away. Add texture, patterns and design details to the helmet, jacket and trousers. Use a sharp pencil line to darken and refine the remaining outlines. Use flat shading and dark contour lines to build tone on the tires, neck and goggles. With a soft touch, add shading to the trees and ground.

**INTERESTING FACT** → In 2008, BMX racing became an Olympic sport.

# BREAKDANCING

*This exciting dance style began in the South Bronx of New York City in the 1970s as part of hip-hop culture and the urban-music scene. Breakdancing combines improvized freestyle dancing with a range of rehearsed athletic steps and poses.*

## Before you begin

The key feature of this drawing is the strong shapes made by the body. Notice how it seems to be divided into three parts: the head, the torso and the legs. Use steps 1 and 2 to get these three parts roughly sketched, and the rest of the drawing will flow easily.

## Step

Use a ruler to sketch the baseline. Using a clock-face, add the other two ruled guidelines. Sketch circles for the head, shoulder and bottom. Checking distances with your thumb and a pencil, sketch in the remaining ellipses. Add a short line for the chin and shoulder.

## Step 2

Add guidelines for the facial features. Sketch the arms and hand shapes. Lightly sketch the torso shape and waist lines. Starting with the cuffs of the trousers, add lines for the legs. Add details for the shoes.

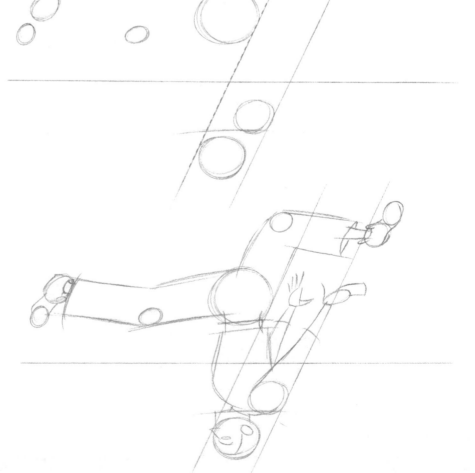

## Step ③

Erase any unnecessary lines. With a sharp pencil, refine the details of the face and head. Add a wriggly line for the top. Pressing lightly, add softer lines for its folds and contours. Noticing the folds in the trousers, refine the outline using longer, flowing lines. Refine the fingers and hands. Add details to the shoes and ankles. Softly sketch movement lines (so the figure looks like he is spinning) and begin to build a floor shadow with cross-hatching.

## Step ④

Refine your line work with a sharp pencil. Vary its pressure to help show different body parts. Use soft flat shading on the trousers, skin and floor. Build texture and darker tones using flat shading, cross-hatching and contour lines. Leave highlights to show folds and to give volume. With your eraser, add movement lines to the top and arms. Notice how the floor shadow is darkest just beneath his skull. Darken the hair and add details to the shoes.

### DRAWING TIP

Changing pencil pressure, contour lines and line work can help show a variety of fabrics and materials.

Show different fabrics by using a variety of line work

Show different fabrics by using a variety of line work

**INTERESTING FACT** → Hip-hop music is made up of a number of looped-together "breaks". A "break" is the moment in a song when just the bass is playing, with no vocals or melody, resulting in the name "breakdancing".

# GYMNASTICS

*Modern gymnastics evolved from exercises used by the Ancient Greeks, including skills for mounting and dismounting a horse. Exercises are now performed on a horse–like device called the pommel horse, as well as on uneven bars, balance beams, a high bar, parallel bars, still rings and the floor.*

## Before you begin

The key elements in this drawing are the gymnast's dynamic pose and his muscles. Take your time with steps 1 and 2 when sketching the pose and body shapes.

## Step 1

Sketch the main three guidelines using a ruler and a clock-face. Use your thumb and a pencil to mark the location of the wrists, elbows, waist, knees and ankles. Drawing lightly, sketch the head shapes. Working on one arm at a time, sketch ellipses for the shoulder, bicep and forearm and draw shapes for the hands. Add ellipses for the waist, knees and feet.

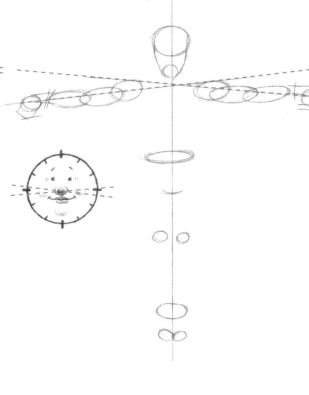

## Step 2

Add ellipses for the rings and lines for their hand straps. Still drawing lightly, add lines for the hair and face. Sketch lines for the neck and the U-shaped neck-line of the top. Sketch the two arm-shapes of the top. Add lines to the torso, noticing how it begins under the shoulder ellipses and tapers down to the waist. Sketch other line work for the torso. Lightly draw the leg shapes. Add contour lines for the costume pattern.

## Step 3

Erase any unnecessary lines. Refine the overall shapes and the outline with a sharp pencil, smoothing the curves as you go. Spend some time detailing the head, face and hands. Refine the muscles of the arms using a strong outline, then add softer contour lines to show volume and muscle tone. Add soft contour lines to the hand straps, feet and torso. Lightly sketch the audience, stadium roof and scoreboard.

*Fade the line work to suggest the straps continue*

*Leave a gap*

*Leave a gap*

## Step 4

Erase any unnecessary lines. Refine all outlines with a sharp pencil and detail the face, hands and rings. Add soft, flat shading to the head, neck and arms. Build the tone of the costume using flat shading and contour lines. Leave highlights along the edge of the costume to show volume. Leave the stripe around the costume white.

INTERESTING FACT → The aim of a gymnast when using "still rings" is to perform a routine showing balance, strength, grace and dynamic motion while preventing the rings themselves from swinging.

# ROCK-CLIMBING

*Clambering up and over rocks goes with the territory for mountaineers. And it's from mountain-climbing that the sport of rock-climbing came into its own. Rock-climbing can be done aided by harness, rope and anchor systems (top-roping, lead-climbing) or with just the hands and feet (bouldering, free solo climbing).*

## Before you begin

This drawing's feature is the combination of the climber's dynamic posture and his muscular body. There is also tension, created by the climber hanging onto the rock by the tips of his fingers!

## Step 1

Using a clock-face and ruler, sketch the two main guidelines. Plot the distances of the remaining shapes along these lines, using your thumb and pencil. Sketch the main ellipses for the head and bottom and add the shoulder ellipse. Sketch the bent leg's thigh-line and add the small ellipse at each end. Add the cuff shapes and boot ellipses, one foot at a time, noticing how one sits almost directly above the other.

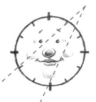

## Step 2

Sketch lines for the hair, face, jaw and shoulder. Using your thumb and pencil, plot the distance of the outstretched hand. Sketch an ellipse for this hand, ensuring it is slightly higher than the shoulder ellipse. Lightly draw the remaining shapes for this arm and an ellipse for the other hand. Add remaining lines for the climber's right arm and shoulder. Sketch the large ellipse for the armhole of the top and lines for the torso. Add lines for the shoes and ankles of both legs. Now draw the trousers, one leg at a time. Sketch in a rock and a flying bird.

## Step ③

Erase any unnecessary lines and soften any rough line work. With a sharp pencil, refine the overall outline, smoothing the curved lines of muscles and clothing as you go. Detail the hair and facial features, giving the face a determined expression. Begin to add soft contour lines to show folds in the trousers and shadows on the rock. Add line work for the fingers on both hands.

*Angled eyebrows help show determination*

*Leave a gap*

## Step ④

Use a combination of flat shading and contour lines to build shadow areas and textures. Press heavily to build the darkest areas, such as the hair, top, chalk bag and shoes. Leave highlights on the trousers. Darken the outlines with a sharp pencil and refine the facial details. Add cross-hatching to the background to create a rocky texture. Create soft shapes for clouds and a distant horizon.

**INTERESTING FACT** ➡ Gymnastic chalk, a powder carried by many rock-climbers, improves grip by absorbing sweat.

# SKATEBOARDING

*The popularity of skateboarding grew rapidly in the 1960s with Californian surfers riding boards adapted for land during times when the surf was flat. Skateboarding is no longer just a recreational activity, but also a competitive sport, a mode of transport and, to some riders, a way of life.*

## Before you begin

The two main elements of this drawing are the amount of detail and the skateboarder's exciting pose. It looks difficult, but take your time with each step and you will surprise yourself with how simple it can be.

## Step 1

Using a clock-face to check the angle, rule the two main guidelines. Lightly sketch a horizontal line for the face. Sketch the helmet and neck ellipses. Add lines for the chin and neck. Use your thumb and a pencil to mark the location of the foot, knees and wrist ellipses and sketch them. Add a curved line touching the knee ellipse. Add both elbow ellipses and the two remaining lines for the arm and leg.

## Step 2

Keep drawing lightly. Working on one part at a time, add lines for the helmet and face. Sketch the chest shape and the lower arm and elbow-pad. Add the baseline. Sketch loose lines for the trousers. Add lines to complete the right bent leg and the knee-pad. Refine the upper boot. Add shapes for the skateboard and lines for the upper hand, arm and elbow-pad. Sketch other lines for the T-shirt and the remaining leg and knee-pad. Phew! That's a lot of detail.

*Don't forget to add the second boot*

*This elbow sits behind the knee-pad*

## Step ③

Soften or erase any unnecessary lines. With a sharp pencil, refine the overall outline, adding smooth, curved lines as you go. Refine the folds in the fabric, and the facial features and hair. Work your way through the entire drawing, refining and adding details. Add soft contour lines to show volume and texture. Sketch a sun or another design on the T-shirt. Lightly draw the rest of the skate ramp and the background.

*Leave a gap*

*Leave a highlight*

## Step ④

Use flat shading and contour lines to build volume and texture. Leave space around the lower knee-pad to make it appear closer. To make other areas seem further away, use a lighter pencil pressure. With a sharp pencil, darken the outlines and refine the details. Add movement lines, details to the background and a shadow near the lower hand.

**INTERESTING FACT** → In July 2005, Danny Way jumped over the Great Wall of China on his skateboard, becoming the first person to jump the wall without motorized aid.

# SNOWBOARDING

*Snowboarding developed in the United States in the 1960s and 1970s. It became a Winter Olympic Sport in 1998. This type of skiing, inspired by surfing and skateboarding, uses a single board fitted to the boarder's boots with a special binding.*

## Before you begin

The main feature of this drawing is the movement created by the snow. This is achieved by drawing very little and leaving a lot of white space – a clever trick.

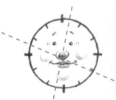

## Step ①

Draw lightly at first. Using a clock-face and ruler, sketch the two main guidelines. Add two head ellipses and a line for the back. Sketch a long curved line and ellipses for the board. Add ellipses for the feet and the hand on the board. Add the remaining lines and shapes for the arm and other hand.

## Step ②

Very lightly and freely sketch the mountain incline and cloud shapes for the snow. Add a few movement lines. Draw in goggles and facial features. Add lines for both arms, then sketch in the jacket and trousers.

## Step

Erase any unnecessary lines. Pressing lightly, add definition to the rocks, snow and landscape in the background. With a sharp pencil, refine the goggles and face. Add texture and pattern to the hat. Define the drawing overall, but don't press too heavily. Add wriggly lines to show folds in the jacket and trousers. Begin to sketch contour lines to give volume to the clothing. Refine the outline of the board and add a small design.

## DRAWING TIP

Hold your pencil loosely and sketch quickly when drawing snow or clouds.

*Build layers of flat shading and cross-hatching*

## Step

Use flat shading and cross-hatching to build the tone of the background, leaving much of the area white. Build the volume and tone of the board, trousers and hat using flat shading and contour lines. With a sharp pencil, refine and darken the outline of the board and rider, leaving some areas soft or white. Swipe your eraser over these areas, and nearby areas, to create white movement lines. Add soft contour lines to clouds. You can add spots of flying snow with a brush and white paint, if you have it.

*Swipe your eraser to create movement lines*

*Leave highlights*

**INTERESTING FACT** → On 2 May 1999, in France, Darren Powell (Australia) reached 125.459mph on his snowboard. In 2006 this was still the highest recorded speed on a snowboard.

# SOCCER

Soccer is a fast-paced ball-sport with eleven players in a team. It requires great co-ordination and ball-handling skills, as well as a high level of fitness. Soccer players are generally lighter and more agile than players from other football codes.

## Before you begin

The main features of this drawing are the dynamic pose and the fact that the player is in mid-air. Take your time setting up the structure in steps 1 and 2 and the rest of the drawing will follow easily.

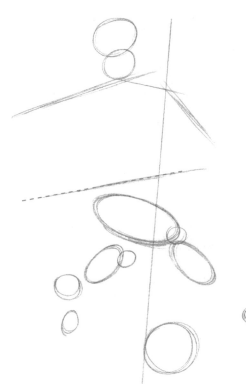

## Step 1

Using your ruler, sketch a near-vertical guideline. Using a clock-face, sketch a line for the waist. Add the other straight lines for the arms. Sketch ellipses for the head. Holding your pencil loosely, sketch the large ellipse for the thigh, followed by the circle for the ball. Add ellipses for the knees, lower legs and feet.

## Step 2

Drawing lightly and beginning at the head, add a hairline and small ellipses for the face. Add lines for the ear, neck and collar. Using your thumb and pencil to plot distance, sketch the outline of the player's top. Add shapes for the hands and arms and sketch the shorts. Focusing on one at a time, add lines for the legs, leg-pads and boots. Sketch a horizon line and a baseline for the ball. Add lines for the ball's stitching pattern.

# Step ③

Erase any unnecessary lines and soften rough line work. Add softly drawn ellipses for the crowd in the background. Add some movement lines and grass. Use flat shading and contours to create dark, curly hair. Sharpen your pencil and begin to refine the drawing. Use heavy lines for the dark eyes and hairline. Spend some time on the face, giving it an observant expression. Use wriggly lines to help show folds in the clothing. Use smooth lines for the arms and face outlines. Add contour lines to the ball and details to the boots and fingers to each hand.

*Leave highlights to give volume*

# Step ④

Refine the drawing with a sharp pencil and a heavy outline. Use flat shading and contour lines to darken the skin. Press heavily for the boots and hair. Darken the facial features. Leave the collar, shorts and leg-pads mainly white, but add contour lines to give them volume. Use flat shading on the top and contour lines to add definition to the folds. Add flat shading and cross-hatching to the grass and soccer ball. Pressing lightly, add more tone and detail to the background.

*Flat shading and contour lines create dark skin*

**INTERESTING FACT** ➔ The term "soccer" originated in England in the 1880s as a slang abbreviation of Association Football. In countries where it is the most popular football code, this sport is generally known as "football".

cool Things To Draw: Extreme Action

# SURFING

*The art of surfing was first observed by Europeans in Tahiti in 1767. Surfing was a central part of ancient Polynesian culture, with the chief – the most skilled wave rider in the community – owning the best board made from the best tree.*

## Before you begin

Examine the structure of this drawing. It is made up of two main areas: the board and rider, and the waves around them. The first part needs line work and detail, while the second relies more on tone.

## Step 1

Holding your pencil loosely, lightly sketch the three long curved lines for the board and wave. Use your thumb and a pencil to plot distances. Add the ellipse for the head and jaw lines. Sketch lines for the straight arm, adding ellipses for the shoulder and bicep, and lines for the wrist band. Add ellipses for the other arm and two curved lines for the main leg.

## Step 2

Keep sketching lightly. Add the large wave shape and sketch in smaller wave lines. Add facial features and hair. Draw lines for the back and shorts. Sketch each leg and foot, one at a time. Add lines for the bent arm and shapes for the hand and fingers. Sketch the other hand and fingers. Give the board a curved tip and begin to create its decorative design.

# Step 3

Erase or soften any unnecessary lines. Using a sharp pencil, refine the elements of the surfer and his board. Add flowing lines for his hair and use smooth flowing line work for his muscles. Add an ankle strap and contour lines to show muscle tone in the legs and arms. Begin to add flat shading and contour lines to the board and water.

# Step 4

Refine your drawing. Build layers of flat shading and heavy contour lines for the water. Add flowing wavy lines for the effect of flowing water, leaving white areas around the rider so he stands out. Leave most of the wave's crest white, adding only soft, curly line work. Sketch movement lines behind the rider and a dark shadow below the board. Add flat shading and soft contour lines to his body, hair and shorts. Sketch a small shadow near his foot. Swipe your eraser over some of the drawing to create white movement lines.

Leave white space

Swipe your eraser to create movement lines

**INTERESTING FACT** → It's possible to surf in a river. When a large amount of water flows back on itself – over a submerged rock for example – it creates a wave, which is sometimes surfable.

# WRESTLING

*Wrestling is a show-sport that involves two unarmed persons. Each wrestler tries to gain control over the other without causing serious harm. The winner is typically the wrestler who pins their opponent's shoulders to the ground for a count of 10 seconds.*

## Before you begin

The main elements in this drawing are the posture of the larger fighter and the way he leans to the right, giving his actions movement and power. This is a complex drawing, so use your thumb and pencil to help plot distances, and take your time.

## Step

Using your ruler and a clock-face, sketch the main guideline. This line will be used to attach most of the main shapes. Drawing lightly, sketch the horizontal waistline and a baseline. Use your ruler to add the other long vertical guideline, ensuring it is at a slightly different angle to the first. Add a circle for the wrestler's bottom. Add ellipses for the chest, shoulders and head, and lines for his strong jaw. Lightly sketch ellipses for each leg and foot.

## Step 2

Focus on the larger wrestler first. Add facial details, hair and lines for his shoulders. Sketch an ellipse and curved line for his bicep. Add lines for his torso and waist. Sketch his other arm and hand. Add lines for his leg, still holding your pencil loosely. Now work on the smaller wrestler. Sketch in his bottom and add ellipses for his legs. Draw shapes for his boots, one at a time. Add a circle for his head, lines for his neck and shapes for his lower arm. Sketch lines for his bent arm and add the torso lines.

# Step ③

Erase or soften any unnecessary lines. With a sharp pencil, refine the overall outlines and smooth the curved lines. Add a fierce expression to the large wrestler's face. Darken his eyes and give movement to his hair. Add details to his fingers, shorts, knee-pads and boots. Lightly sketch in the wrestling-ring ropes and a floor. Keeping a sharp pencil, refine the body parts of the smaller wrestler. Add details to his hands, face, hair, boots and arms. Add contour lines throughout the drawing to show muscle tone and give volume.

*Give him a fierce expression*

*Leave highlights to show volume*

# Step ④

Softly sketch an audience, giving them funny faces. Use flat shading to add tone and create volume to your wrestlers. Build the dark areas of the boots, shorts and hair using heavy contour lines and shading. Build muscle tone with shading and contour lines, leaving highlights to create volume. Create a shadow on the floor using cross-hatching and tone. Add tone and texture to the wrestling-ring ropes and post. Refine all the outlines and details of the drawing using a sharp pencil.

**INTERESTING FACT** → Shuai Jiao, a wrestling style originating in China over 4000 years ago, is arguably the most ancient example of wrestling. Wrestling is also mentioned in the Bible's Old Testament.

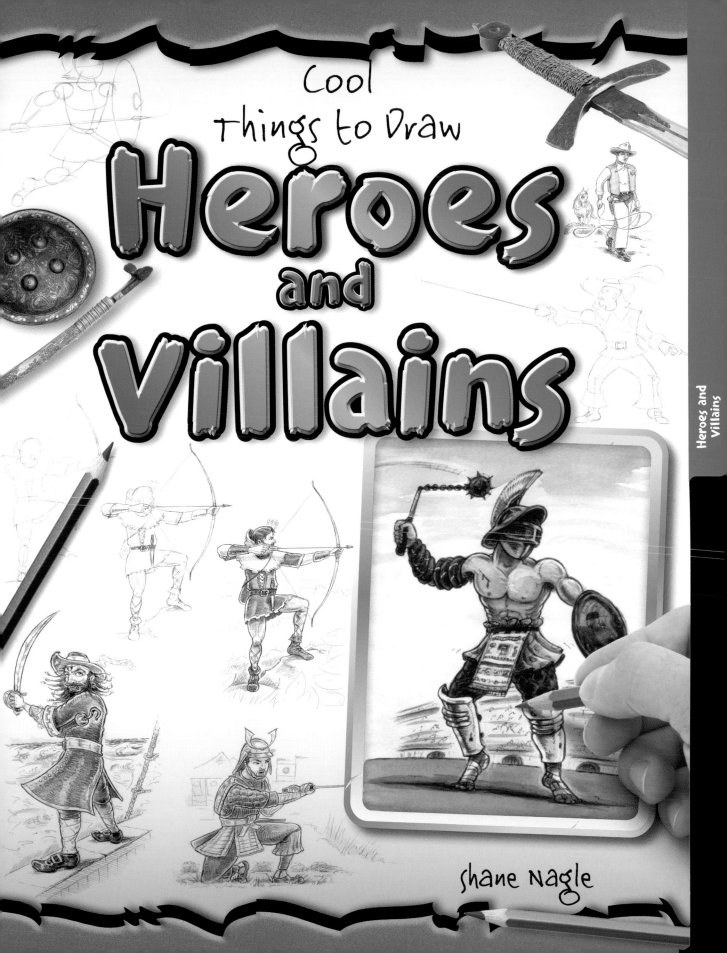

Cool Things to Draw

# Heroes
## and
# Villains

Shane Nagle

Heroes and Villains

# Cool Things to Draw

# Heroes
## and
# Villains

# INTRODUCTION

*Stories of action-packed battles between heroes and villains are common around the world, and many date back thousands of years.*

*Enjoy learning how to draw characters from both sides of this battle. You'll discover lots of muscles, weapons, costumes, and exciting postures. So sharpen that pencil and draw!*

## THINGS YOU WILL NEED

- A #2 pencil
- A clean eraser
- Sheets of paper
- A pencil sharpener
- A ruler
- A sense of humor and a positive attitude. Enjoy!

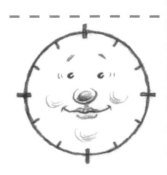

## Using the clock-face

This fun tip will help you sketch lines at different angles. *Look at the line you want to draw.*
*Now imagine that line on a clock-face: where would it point?*
*Draw a line on your page, matching the angle on the imaginary clock-face.*

## Drawing guidelines

When drawing your heroes and villains, pay attention to these things:

1   Each drawing begins with basic shapes and guidelines
2   Always draw lightly at first
3   Focus on one part of the drawing at a time
4   Build texture and volume in layers
5   Experiment with different pencil techniques as you go along
6   Practice, practice, practice!

# Step-by-step drawing

Each drawing is made by following steps. Read through all the steps carefully before you begin, then follow them one at a time until your drawing is done. Don't worry if your drawing looks different to the examples; all artists find their own style and your skills will improve with practice.

**Step 1**  **Step 2**  **Step 3**  **Step 4**

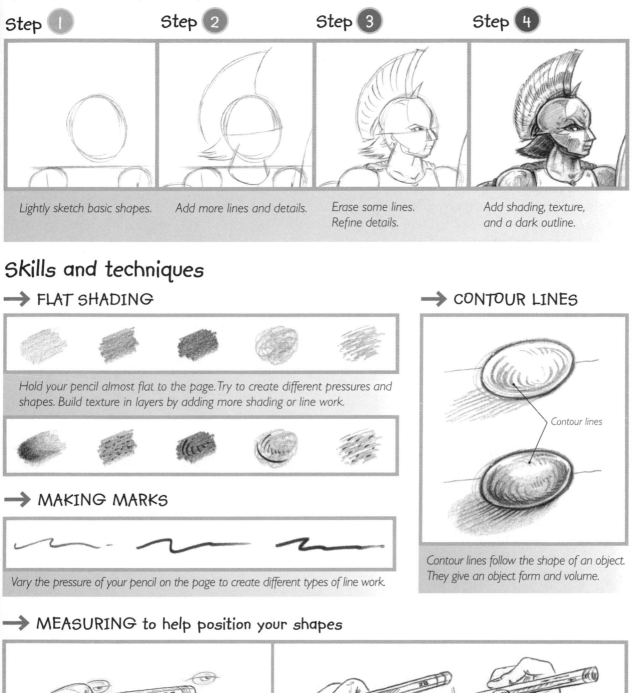

Lightly sketch basic shapes.   Add more lines and details.   Erase some lines. Refine details.   Add shading, texture, and a dark outline.

# Skills and techniques

## → FLAT SHADING

Hold your pencil almost flat to the page. Try to create different pressures and shapes. Build texture in layers by adding more shading or line work.

## → MAKING MARKS

Vary the pressure of your pencil on the page to create different types of line work.

## → CONTOUR LINES

Contour lines

Contour lines follow the shape of an object. They give an object form and volume.

## → MEASURING to help position your shapes

Use a pencil like a ruler, marking the distance with your thumb. Mark that length with another pencil on your paper.

# ADVENTURER

*Many dangerous quests and battles have been won by heroic women. This adventurer has seen amazing things on her quests to find ancient treasures from lost civilizations. She is intelligent, resourceful, holds a black-belt in Karate, can speak seven languages, and is as fit as an acrobat.*

## Before you begin

One important element of this drawing is the angle of the adventurer's body. Use a clock-face to help make the ruled guideline, and then construct the drawing around it. Measure the position of the adventurer's feet and hands using your thumb and pencil. Pay attention to the facial expressions.

## Step ①

Always press lightly at first. Draw a long ruled guideline and a shorter line for the shoulders. Use a clock-face to get the correct angles. Add an ellipse for the head, first checking the size and angle. Sketch a curved waistline and small ellipses for the knee and right foot, using your pencil and thumb to measure them. Add lines for the torso, neck, and arm, and an ellipse for the hand.

## Step ②

Observe the shapes used to make the right leg and sketch them lightly. Sketch an ellipse for the elbow. Add the knife and lines for both arms. Observing the direction of the face, sketch a guideline for the eyes, and then ellipses and lines for the facial features and hair. Add ellipses for the second foot and the outlines of the clothing.

# Step 3

Erase most of the ruled guidelines. Still sketching lightly, draw the back leg, belt, boots, gun, and holster. Erase some of the ellipse shape used for the head. Sketch lines for the chin and cheek. Add the fingers, wrist bands, and other costume details. With a sharper pencil, begin to refine some of the line work. Erase any unnecessary lines.

# Step 4

Using a sharp pencil, create a strong outline. Build the volume of this drawing using contour lines and shading. Use a variety of pencil pressures to show the different textures. Pay attention to the hair and the expression on the face, adding details with a freshly sharpened pencil. Add a vine and lightly draw in mountains, some trees, and a cloudy sky.

INTERESTING FACT → With the right training, a woman is easily able to defeat a man in hand-to-hand combat, even if she is smaller in size.

78

# GLADIATOR

*The word gladiator comes from the Latin word* gladius, *meaning "short sword." Gladiators were professional fighters who battled to entertain the public, politicians, and rulers of ancient Rome. They used swords, shields, and other weapons. But unlike sports and entertainment today, these fights were often to the death, and sometimes involved wild animals and slaves.*

## Before you begin

The gladiator appears to be about to strike with his weapon. This effect is caused not just by having his arm in the air but also by the angle of his head, torso, and legs, and by the way his feet touch the ground. Notice that some of the construction lines used for the legs are slightly curved.

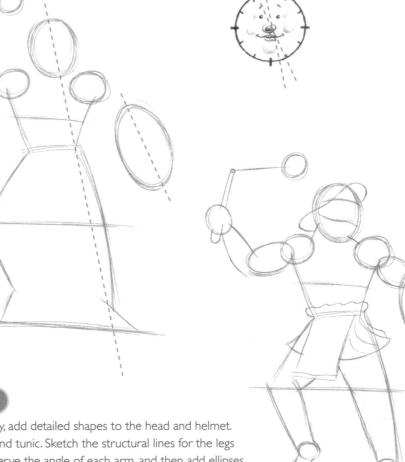

## Step ①

Start with a larger ellipse for the shield, and then sketch the remaining smaller ones for the head, shoulders, and hand. Check the distances using your thumb and a pencil, then add construction lines for the legs and torso and a baseline. Be careful to set the lines for the feet at the correct angle to the baseline.

## Step ②

Drawing lightly, add detailed shapes to the head and helmet. Draw a belt and tunic. Sketch the structural lines for the legs and feet. Observe the angle of each arm, and then add ellipses and lines for the arms and the weapon.

# Step 3

Erase any unnecessary lines. Add a brush shape and other details to the helmet. Erase or soften the lines of the torso, then draw over them to make the torso more muscular. Sketch rings of ellipses on the shield. Add the leg armor shapes and more details to the feet. Create curves for the padding on the raised arm and add the details for the hand and weapon. Refine the drawing with slightly darker line work.

## DRAWING TIP

To help give an object volume, leave a highlight (or gap) along the edge of your shading or contour lines.

Leave a gap along the edge

Leave a gap along the edge

# Step 4

Build the volume of the body with layers of flat-shading, contour lines, and pencil marks. Add detail to the clothing, armor and shield, sketching scratches, dents, and dirt as well as texture and patterns to the fabric. Define the hair of the brush, the helmet, and the wrapping on the feet. Create padded pants using shading and contour lines, leaving highlights along the edge of each diamond shape. Use heavy, sharp pencil line work for the cuts and other details. Add a shadow on the ground and lightly sketch the colosseum of people in the background.

INTERESTING FACT → Many popular gladiators had sponsors. They appeared on billboards and would endorse products before their fights.

cool Things To Draw: Heroes & Villains

# GREEK WARRIOR

*Ancient Greek warfare was dominated by the courage, skill, and strength of the foot soldiers. These highly disciplined warriors were famous in battle for the use of a phalanx formation, where fifty or more soldiers would advance in lines, their shields locked together to create a protective wall and their long spears thrust forward like a porcupine.*

## Before you begin

The key elements in this drawing are the position of the legs and spear-arm and the detailed and shiny armor. All elements are built gradually, using lines, ellipses, and shading. Approach the drawing of your Greek warrior one step at a time and you will soon be proud of the result.

## Step ①

Draw lightly, sketch the spear line using a ruler and a clock-face. Measuring the distances with a pencil and your thumb, sketch slightly curved lines for the leg, baseline, and torso. Holding your pencil loosely, sketch the ellipses for the head, shoulders, and foot.

## Step ②

Using your thumb and pencil to plot its position, sketch the spear hand. Add lines and an ellipse for the arm. Draw lines for the helmet, hair, and neck and a second ruled line for the spear. Sketch the ellipse for the shield and lines for the spearhead, shield-tip, chest, belt, and tunic. Add guidelines for the legs and feet, being careful with the placement of the rear foot.

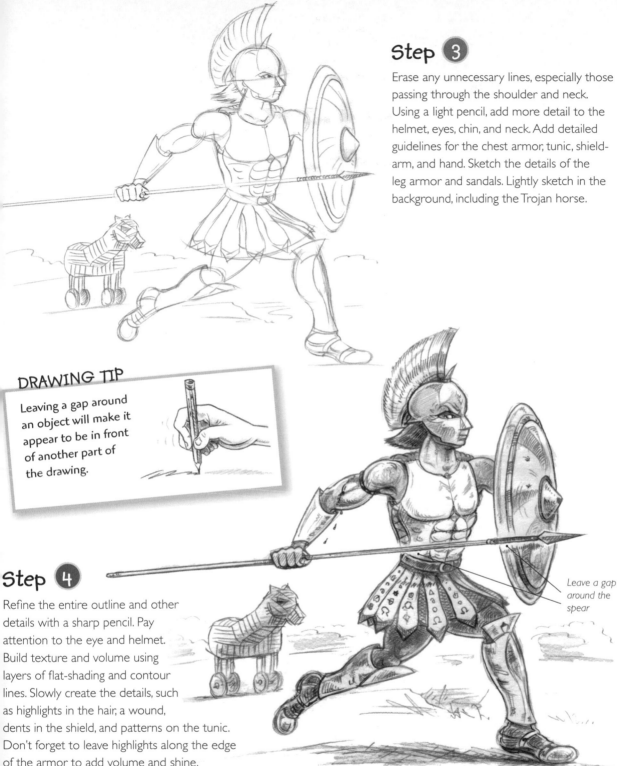

## Step ③

Erase any unnecessary lines, especially those passing through the shoulder and neck. Using a light pencil, add more detail to the helmet, eyes, chin, and neck. Add detailed guidelines for the chest armor, tunic, shield-arm, and hand. Sketch the details of the leg armor and sandals. Lightly sketch in the background, including the Trojan horse.

## DRAWING TIP

Leaving a gap around an object will make it appear to be in front of another part of the drawing.

## Step ④

Refine the entire outline and other details with a sharp pencil. Pay attention to the eye and helmet. Build texture and volume using layers of flat-shading and contour lines. Slowly create the details, such as highlights in the hair, a wound, dents in the shield, and patterns on the tunic. Don't forget to leave highlights along the edge of the armor to add volume and shine.

*Leave a gap around the spear*

**INTERESTING FACT** ➞ In Greek mythology, the brave and strong hero Achilles died when he was shot in the heel by an arrow. A person's only weakness has become known as their *Achilles heel*.

cool Things To draw: Heroes & Villains

# KNIGHT

HARD

*A knight served a lord or a king in medieval times. In times of war, a knight was expected to fight. Knights followed a code of chivalry, meaning they had to act with honor, bravery, courtesy, and loyalty.*

## Before you begin

This drawing begins with a simple structure, mostly made from straight lines. Remember to hold your pencil gently and keep your arm loose as you sketch guidelines. Use a clock-face and your thumb and pencil to plot the position of the lines.

## Step 1

Sketch a baseline, using a clock-face to create the correct angle. Draw the other straight lines of the drawing's simple structure, noticing the difference in their angles. Lightly sketch the different sizes and shapes of the ellipses.

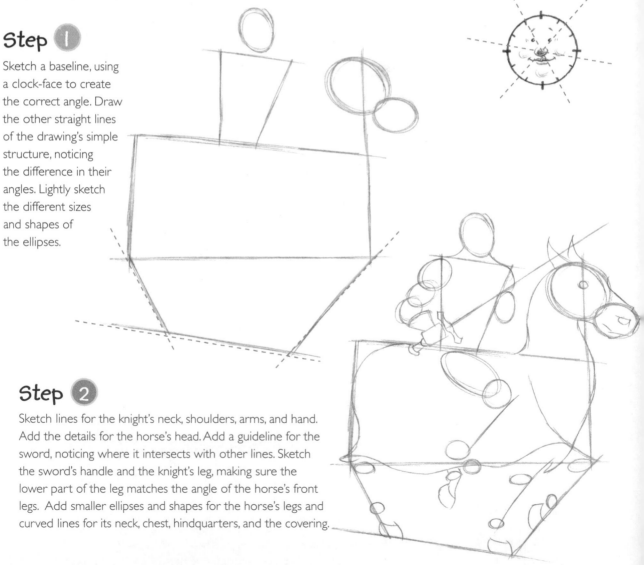

## Step 2

Sketch lines for the knight's neck, shoulders, arms, and hand. Add the details for the horse's head. Add a guideline for the sword, noticing where it intersects with other lines. Sketch the sword's handle and the knight's leg, making sure the lower part of the leg matches the angle of the horse's front legs. Add smaller ellipses and shapes for the horse's legs and curved lines for its neck, chest, hindquarters, and the covering.

# Step ③

Erase any unnecessary lines, especially the straight guidelines. Working on one element at a time, use a sharp pencil to detail the arms and sword, and add a shield to the left arm. Refine the helmet, chest armor, tunic, saddle, and leg. Add details to the horse's head such as hair, eyes, mane, bridle, and reins. Sketch a pattern of squares on the covering and add the tail. Refine the legs and hooves.

## DRAWING TIP

Leave highlights to show volume. Imagine the sun is shining down, casting shadows and creating highlights.

Leave a gap around the sword

Leave a highlight

Leave a highlight

Leave a highlight

Leave a highlight

# Step ④

Using heavy, sharp line work, darken the outlines. Create the details of the armor and clothing. Build volume and texture in layers, using flat shading and contour lines, and a variety of pencil marks and pressures. Leave a gap around the sword to show that it is in the foreground. Add a pattern to the bridle and covering. Use cross-hatching to create a shadow on the ground and sketch a castle in the background.

**INTERESTING FACT** → Boys could train to be knights, becoming pages when they turned six and squires when they were 14 or 15. They became knights when they mastered their training and they could also be dubbed knights on the battlefield by the king or their lord.

# MUSKETEER

*A musketeer was a member of the French royal guards in the 17th and 18th centuries. Their main role was to protect the members of the royal families. Musketeers were first regarded as junior soldiers and lower members of the nobility, but they soon gained a reputation for their skill and fighting spirit and they became popular favorites of the royal court.*

## Before you begin

The key element to this drawing is the steady posture of the musketeer. This is created with a simple skeleton structure for the legs. Notice that the main guideline for the sword helps to set the positions of the ellipses and lines for the arms and torso.

## Step ①

Using a clock-face and a ruler, sketch the main line for the sword, the baseline, and the skeleton lines for the legs. Using your thumb and pencil to measure, lightly sketch the ellipses and circles for the head and arms. Add lines for the torso, neck, and belt and shapes for the big boots.

## Step ②

Sketch in a hat with a feather, hair, and some facial features. Thicken the main line where the sword is by adding another long line. Add details to the arms and hands. Working your way down the body, sketch the pants, and add details to the boots and buckle.

## Step 3

Erase any unnecessary lines. Begin to refine the drawing using a sharp pencil. Add details to the face, head, and hat. Use a wiggly line to create the folds in the fabric of the pants. With a soft pencil, begin to add contour lines to the costume to create volume. Lightly sketch the background elements and other details, like frills on the cuffs, and a flower arrangement in his hat.

### DRAWING TIP

For soft shadows, such as on the forehead, only use flat shading. For heavier shadows, such as under the hat, use flat shading and line work.

*Flat shading only*

*Use flat shading and line work*

## Step 4

Using sharp, heavy line work, darken all outlines. Build the texture of the costume, hair, and shadow areas in layers, using lots of flat shading and heavy contour lines. Leave the collars and cuffs mostly white. Darken the facial features with a very sharp pencil. Add a soft shadow and tone to the ground and landscape.

INTERESTING FACT → The word "musketeer" comes from a long-barreled gun called a musket. However, the musketeers in the well-known novel **The Three Musketeers** were famous for their skill with swords, and didn't use a musket anywhere in the story.

# NINJA

*Ninja were Japanese assassins, trained to move and strike without being seen or heard. The word ninja translates as "the skill of going unperceived." Ninja were used for missions such as spying, assassination, and scouting: tasks that were regarded as dishonorable for the warrior samurai.*

## Before you begin

The key element of this drawing is the dark costume. To create this effect, begin with layers of flat shading. You will need to press heavily with your pencil and you can experiment with contour lines and pencil marks. Notice that leaving a gap around the sword makes it look like it is glowing.

## Step 1

Using a clock-face and a ruler, sketch the baseline. Add a large ellipse for the leg. Measuring distances using your thumb and a pencil, sketch the head ellipse and the other guidelines, ensuring that most are slightly curved.

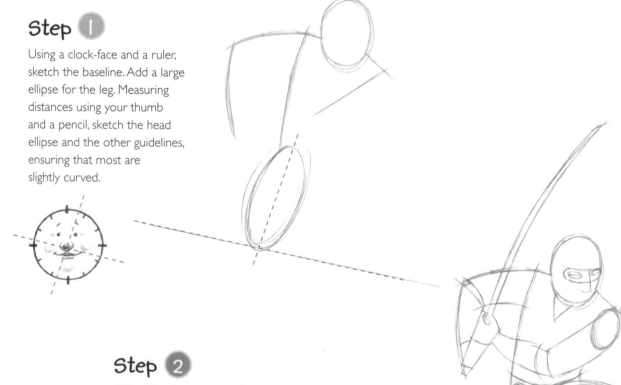

## Step 2

Starting at the elbows, sketch lines for the arms, shoulder, and hands. Add two long curved lines for the sword. Sketch shapes for the eyes and face, and add a large ellipse for the other thigh, and another for the leg and foot.

## Step 3

Erase or soften any unnecessary lines. With a sharp pencil, begin to refine the overall outline of the drawing. Take care to use a variety of line styles, such as wiggly lines to show folds in the sleeves, softer contour lines to show volume, and dark cross-hatching to build texture. Define the eyes and hands. Sketch in the supporting leg and add other details to the costume details.

### DRAWING TIP

To help show definition in a dark drawing, leave highlights of gray instead of white.

*Use cross-hatching to build texture*

*Leave highlights of gray (not white)*

## Step 4

Using sharp, heavy line work, darken all the outlines. Build the dark costume with layers of flat shading, followed by a variety of heavy contour lines. Leave gray highlights around the left arm and a white highlight around the sword. Add cross-hatching to create the shadow on the ground. Press heavily to build texture in dark shadowed areas.

**INTERESTING FACT** → Ninja used gunpowder, smoke bombs, and firecrackers to either create a diversion to help them escape, or for a surprise attack.

88

# PIRATE

*In the days of the sailing ship, pirates were the blood-thirsty thieves of the unchartered seas. Pirates were common along the shores of Africa and in the Caribbean, where they would attack ships that were taking supplies to trade with the settlements there.*

## Before you begin

The challenge in this drawing is creating the detailed face and getting the perspective used to show his legs and feet right. Take your time when building the haggard, toothless face, and remember the main rule of perspective: the smaller things are, the further away they seem to be.

## Step 1

Using a clock-face and ruler, sketch two ruled guidelines. Sketch ellipses for the head, hook, and ankle, using your thumb and a pencil to mark their position. Add other shapes to the foot. Lightly sketch the outline of the jacket and add shapes for the sword hand.

## Step 2

Sketch the base of the hook and add lines for the outstretched arm and sword. Sketch the front leg and the details of the front shoe. Add lines to the opening at the back of the jacket. Observe the difference between the size and shape of the two legs and feet as you sketch the ellipses and shapes for the rear leg and shoe. Observe the face. Note the angle of the eyes and the difference in their size. Sketch the hat and the shapes used on the face.

## Step 3

Erase any unnecessary lines. Refine the drawing using a sharp pencil, adding details to the face and hair. Create wrinkles in the leggings, jacket, and belt using line work. Sketch the wooden side of the ship. Add contour lines and other details, such as the fingers, a hook, buttons, and a frilly shirt. Add details to the sword, leggings, and shoes.

Shape the face with strong outlines

Use a variety of lines

Leave highlight around hook

Soft line work makes this fabric look delicate

### DRAWING TIP

To create a windy scene, show the effect wind has on other objects, such as hair and fabric.

## Step 4

Using sharp, heavy line work, darken the main outlines. Build layers of flat shading and add heavy contour lines to the hair, costume, and boots. Leave highlights to show volume and shine. Darken the facial features, and add details to the costume and shoes. Add shading to the side of the ship and the background. Build the sea using soft, swirling contour lines.

INTERESTING FACT ➡ One of the most famous pirates in literature is Long John Silver from *Treasure Island*. Common ideas about pirates came from this novel, including a treasure map marked with an X, a deserted tropical island, and a one-legged pirate with a parrot on his shoulder.

cool Things To Draw: Heroes & Villains

# ROBIN HOOD

*Robin Hood was an outlaw in medieval England who fought with his band of Merry Men against the evil Sheriff of Nottingham. He lived in Sherwood Forest and was popular with the people because he stole from the rich to give to the poor.*

## Before you begin

The key element to this drawing is the strong shape made by the arms and the bow and arrow. Use a ruler to help draw these lines. Keep your arm loose when sketching the long, curved lines used for the bow.

## Step 1

Rule a horizontal arrow-line. Using a clock-face and ruler, draw the other three ruled lines. Sketch the different shapes used for each hand. Add more lines and an ellipse for the arms and lines for the bent leg. Measure the size of the bow using your thumb and a pencil and mark it on the string lines.

## Step 2

Add an ellipse for the head and sketch the hood. Draw the bow and the arrow-head, and add details for the hand. Sketch the half-circle shapes for the collar. Lightly draw the outline of the costume shape and belt. Plot the position of the lower foot and draw ellipses for it. Sketch more ellipses for the straight leg. Add ellipses and lines to the bent leg. Sketch a rough outline of the ground.

## Step ③

Erase any unnecessary lines. Sketch the hair and facial features. Using a ruler, darken the arrow using a sharp pencil. Refine the bow, arms, and hands and the details of the costume. Add a dagger and lightly draw a quiver of arrows. Refine the legs, adding strapping to them, and detail the boots. Add contour lines to the costume and body, and detail the rocks.

*Leave gray highlights (not white)*

*Use flat shading to create shadow*

## Step ④

Sketching lightly, add more details to the landscape. Using sharp, heavy line work, darken the outlines. Add sharp, fine line work to his face. Build the dark areas with layers of flat shading and contour lines. Leave some areas of the costume white. Leave gray highlights around the arrow hand so it stands out. Press heavily to build texture in dark shadow areas.

INTERESTING FACT ➡ Robin Hood's skill with a bow was so great that he could split one arrow down the middle with another.

# SAMURAI

*For over 1000 years, the samurai were the military nobility of Japan. They lived and died by a disciplined, spiritual code called "bushido" (meaning "way of the warrior"). Skilled with swords, horses, and bows, these men served their lords.*

## Before you begin

The main challenge with this drawing is creating the elaborate costume, which is made from a variety of materials. Build each type of material using different types of line work and use shading to highlight their differences.

Helmet

Head

## Step 1

Use a ruler to draw the sword and guide lines. Sketch ellipses and circles for the helmet, head, shoulder, and hands. Drawing lightly, add lines for the arm and neck. Sketch the outline of the belt and costume, using a clock-face to check angles. Using your thumb and a pencil, plot the length of the sword.

Add another circle

## Step 2

Add another circle above the helmet for the u-shaped decoration. Sketch more lines on the helmet, including a visor. Add ellipses for the facial features and sketch details to the hands. Draw lines for the rear arm and add lines to the shoulder area. Add rectangular shapes to the costume below the belt. Observing the position of the legs, sketch circles for knees and ellipses for feet. Add curved lines for the trousers and legs.

*Soften unnecessary lines with eraser before refining the face*

## Step ③

Erase or soften any unnecessary lines. Refine all outlines with a sharp pencil. Using a ruler, add a second line to the sword and draw a sharp point at its tip. Refine the face using thin lines and create the u-shape on top of the helmet. Working on one part of the costume at a time, use a variety of line work, contour lines, and cross-hatching to add texture to the tunic, a tie in the belt, and padded arms. Add shading under the helmet, straps on the shoes, and details to the trousers. Lightly sketch in the background.

*Draw lightly*

## Step ④

Build layers of flat-shading to refine each costume part, using different types of shading and contour lines. Leave highlights in the padding. Create a gray highlight around the main arm to help it stand out. Using sharp, heavy pencil line work, darken the main outlines. Add more detail to background and add shading to the grass.

*Don't draw a strong baseline*

**INTERESTING FACT** → *Ronin* (meaning "drifting person") was the name given to a masterless samurai. They roamed the country doing menial tasks or selling themselves as swords-for-hire in exchange for food and shelter.

# SHERIFF

*In the harsh landscape of North America's Wild West, most towns relied on a sheriff for protection from outlaws. The sheriff was elected to maintain law and order. These men were tough and independent leaders who commanded respect by their presence.*

## Before you begin

The structure of this drawing is built from simple guidelines and shapes. Take your time getting the initial structure right and the rest of the drawing will be so much easier.

## Step ①

Use your thumb and pencil to measure and plot distances. Drawing lightly, use a clock-face to sketch an ellipse for the head. Add more lines to the head. Sketch a five-sided shape for the torso and long curved lines for the legs. Add the two hand ellipses and the baseline.

## Step ②

Sketch the brim of the hat and shapes for the face, chin, and neck. Add lines for the vest, cuffs, and holster-belt. Sketch an ellipse for the elbow and add lines for the arm and shirt. Noting their position first, sketch the front and rear boots and trousers. Lightly add an outline of the horse.

Erase unnecessary lines

Note the position of rear boot

# Step ③

Erase any unnecessary lines and soften the points of the hat and the shoulders. Refine the outlines with a sharp pencil. Add folds and wrinkles to the clothing. Use fine, dark lines to detail the face. Sketch four ellipses for the lasso. Detail the hand and boots, and add spurs. Define the handkerchief around his neck and add a badge, buttons, tassels, a gun, and buckles. Add a bush in the background, and legs and the features of the horse.

# Step ④

Sketch the lasso. Darken the main outlines with a sharp pencil. Add layers of flat shading, contour lines, and cross-hatching to the body and clothing. Create soft shading on the face under the hat brim. Darken the boots, leaving gray highlights. Add cross-hatching and scratchy marks to the ground. Add shading and definition to the horse and the background. Leave space around the lasso so it stands out.

Leave space

INTERESTING FACT ➔ A sheriff had the authority to deputize others as temporary lawmen to help catch outlaws. Sometimes they would raise a posse (troop) of men to hunt down criminals on the run.

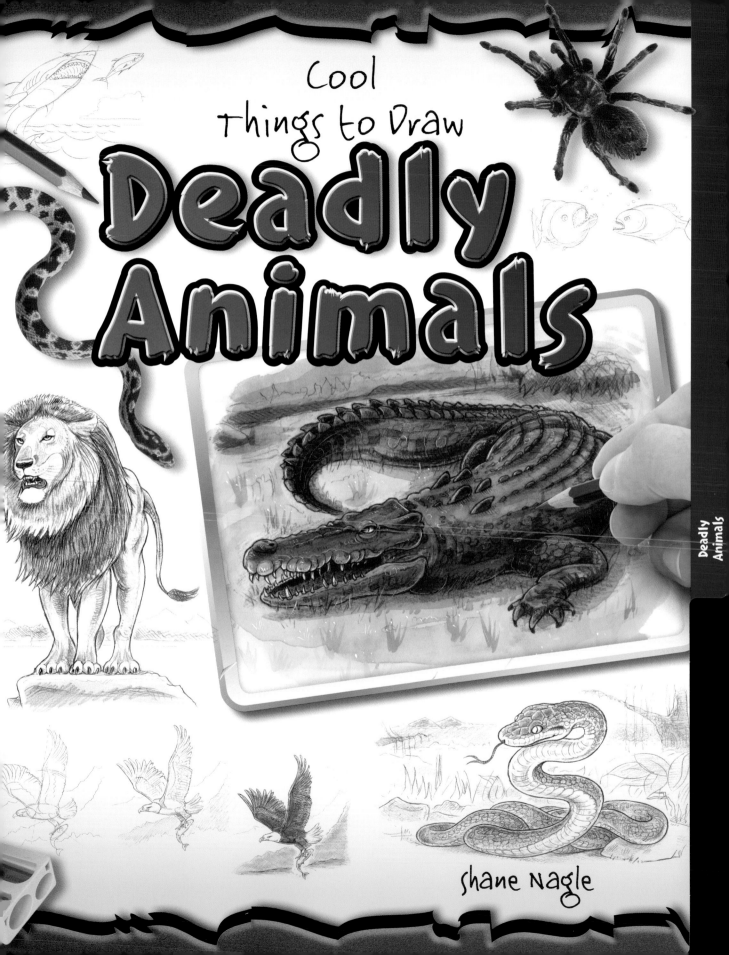

# Cool Things to Draw
# Deadly Animals

# INTRODUCTION

*Look closely at these deadly animals. Behind their sharp claws and fierce eyes, you might see their beauty and realize that, like us, they spend their time playing, eating, sleeping and caring for loved ones. Who knows – should you ever meet, they might be more scared of you than you are of them!*

*There are lots of details in these drawings. Use line work, flat shading and your imagination to create fur, feathers and frighteningly exciting animals!*

## THINGS YOU WILL NEED

- A #2 pencil
- A clean eraser
- Sheets of paper
- A pencil sharpener
- A ruler
- A sense of humor and a positive attitude. Enjoy!

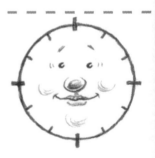

## Using Clock-face

This fun tip will help you sketch lines at different angles.

*Look at the line you want to draw.*

*Now imagine that line on a clock-face: where would it point?*

*Draw a line on your page, matching the angle on the imaginary clock-face.*

## Drawing guidelines

When drawing your deadly animals, pay attention to these things:

1   Each drawing begins with basic shapes and guidelines
2   Always draw lightly at first
3   Focus on one part of the drawing at a time
4   Build texture and volume in layers
5   Experiment with different pencil techniques as you go along
6   Practice, practice, practice!

# Step-by-step drawing

Each drawing is made by following steps. Read through all the steps carefully before you begin, then follow them one at a time until your drawing is done. Don't worry if your drawing looks different to the examples; all artists find their own style and your skills will improve with practice.

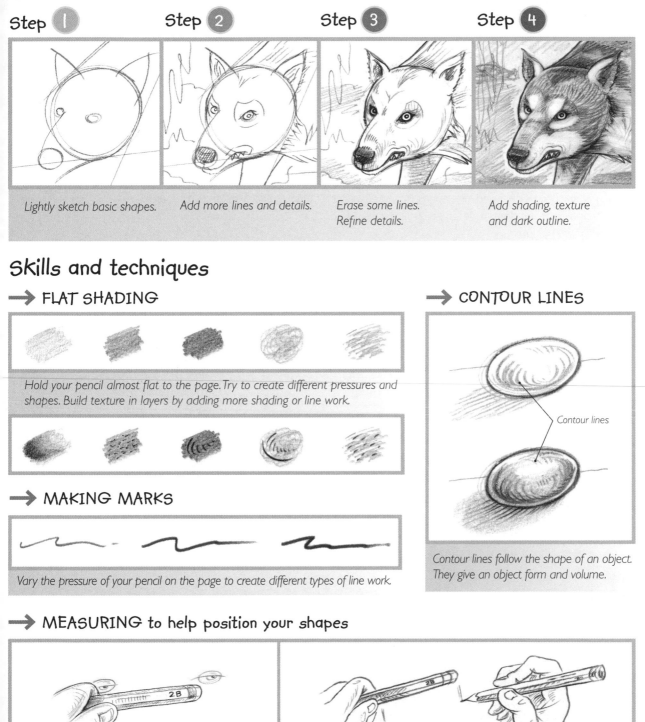

**Step 1**

*Lightly sketch basic shapes.*

**Step 2**

*Add more lines and details.*

**Step 3**

*Erase some lines. Refine details.*

**Step 4**

*Add shading, texture and dark outline.*

# Skills and techniques

## ➜ FLAT SHADING

*Hold your pencil almost flat to the page. Try to create different pressures and shapes. Build texture in layers by adding more shading or line work.*

## ➜ CONTOUR LINES

*Contour lines*

*Contour lines follow the shape of an object. They give an object form and volume.*

## ➜ MAKING MARKS

*Vary the pressure of your pencil on the page to create different types of line work.*

## ➜ MEASURING to help position your shapes

2B

*Use a pencil like a ruler, marking the distance with your thumb. Mark that length with another pencil on your paper.*

cool Things To Draw: Deadly Animals

# CROCODILE

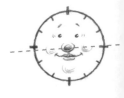

*The saltwater crocodile is the largest living reptile on the planet, with adult males measuring between 16 and 23 feet long and weighing up to 1.3 tons. They are extremely efficient hunters. Once crocodiles snatch their prey, they roll them over and over underwater, disorienting and eventually drowning them.*

## Before you begin

The main feature of this drawing is the detailed crocodile skin. Notice the ridges along its tail and back and the patterns on its neck and legs. Look at those sharp teeth! Steps 2 and 3 are important, as they give each body part the detail it deserves. Use lots of flat shading and contour lines to darken shadow areas and create volume.

## Step 1

Using a clock-face and a ruler, sketch a slightly angled guideline. Add a large circle and then smaller ellipses around it for the legs and feet. Using your thumb and a pencil as a guide, lightly sketch the nose and mouth shapes. Add circles for the eye and lightly sketch the outline of the head and neck.

## Step 2

Still drawing lightly, add long curved lines for the tail. Sketch lines for the rest of the neck and a bumpy line along the snout. Add details to the jaw and mouth and lines for the eyelids and the ridges along the back of the head. Sketch in the five largest blades on the back of the neck. Beginning at these blades, sketch long contour lines for each ridge along the body. Lightly draw an outline for the front leg and shapes for the rear foot and legs. Refine the outline of the whole body.

*Contour lines and ridges
help show volume*

## Step 3

Erase any unnecessary lines. Sharpen your pencil and add teeth to the jaws. Refine and darken the bumpy and textured outline of the jaws and head. Sketch in a tongue and dark line work for the eye. Add ridges to the snout and two lines of raised blades along the tail. Sketch in the smaller raised blades along the back. Lightly draw contour lines on the tail and body to create volume. Add shapes for the skin pattern along the body, snout and tail. Add some grass, noticing how it breaks the outline of the body here and there. Lightly sketch in the background.

### DRAWING TIP

Breaking the outline of an object close to a grassy ground makes it appear to be behind that grass.

## Step 4

Use layers of flat shading, pencil marks and contour lines to build volume and add a leathery texture to the skin. Leave highlights along the edge of all main body parts and outlines. Sharpen your pencil and, pressing heavily, refine the entire bumpy outline of the tail, head and body. Spend time defining the teeth and eye. Darken the inside of the mouth and add tone to some of the skin patterns. Sketch a shadow on the ground and add more grass. Use flat shading and soft contour lines in the background.

*Leave highlights*

*Leave highlights*

### INTERESTING FACT → Crocodiles are believed to be over 200 million years old. They survived the events that caused the extinction of the dinosaurs 65 million years ago.

# BALD EAGLE

*With an average wingspan of 6.5 feet, the bald eagle is the second largest bird of prey in North America. Powerful eyesight (nearly six times sharper than a human's) helps this raptor hunt fish, its main food source. It catches fish by swooping down and snatching them out of the water.*

## Before you begin

The key features of this drawing are its strong V-shape and the eagle's darkly toned feathers. Use steps 1 and 2 to build the structural shapes and outline and then spend time detailing your drawing using lots of flat shading and texture.

## Step 1

Use a ruler and a clock-face to sketch the two main guidelines. Holding your pencil loosely, sketch ellipses for the body and head. Draw in the tail shape and add a thin ellipse for the fish. Checking distances with your thumb and a pencil, sketch the outline of the vertical wing.

## Step 2

Drawing lightly, add the outline of the other wing. Sketch lines for the feathers. On the vertical wing, add feather shapes and refine the outline. Still drawing lightly, add feathers to the tail. Create shapes for the beak and eye and add leg shapes and lines for the shoulder. Sketch the outline of the fish and the lines for the talons. Draw lines for the background.

## DRAWING TIP

When drawing dark feathers or fur, build details and layers of shadow using rapid pencil movements. This will add texture and life to the drawing.

## Step 3

Erase any unnecessary lines. With a sharp pencil, refine the details of the head, starting with the eyes. Notice the smooth curved lines of the body compared with the wriggly lines of the feathers. Refine the outlines of the eagle and the fish. Add feathers to the wings and legs using soft, wriggly lines. Begin to add flat shading on the wings and background.

## Step 4

Refine and darken the main line work with a sharp pencil, varying its pressure to show different body parts. Use soft, flat shading on the beak, eyebrow and neck and strong line work for the eye. Build texture and darker tones for the feathers using layers of flat shading, cross-hatching and contour lines. Leave highlights along the bottom of the body and along the main wing shapes. Add flat shading to give the fish volume and small drops of water. Sketching lightly, create texture in the background. Add faint movement lines with an eraser.

*Leave highlights*

*Leave highlights*

*Add a soft shadow*

## INTERESTING FACT →

Bald eagle nests are used repeatedly over many years, with new materials added each year. Biologists have recorded nests measuring over 9 feet across and weighing 2.2 tons. That's bigger than the average car!

# LION

*Averaging 9 feet in length (with larger males weighing over 550 pounds), lions are the second largest cat. The lion's powerfully built body enables it to deliver forepaw blows heavy enough to break a zebra's back. Although it will gorge itself after a kill, eating 45 to 65 pounds of meat, a lion will also hold a posture that tells nearby animals that it is not hunting.*

## Before you begin

Most of the impact of this drawing comes from the head and mane. The lion's mane is simple to draw, so spend time on the face, giving your lion a confident and powerful expression.

## Step 1

Sketch the two main guidelines using a ruler and a clock-face. Lightly sketch a baseline and a rock shape. Add three ellipses for the paws. Using your thumb and pencil to plot distances, create the main head ellipse. Sketch the outline of the "beard", and then the outline for the mane. Add the smaller ellipses for the leg and tail. Sketch the ellipses for the lower jaw, nose and eyes and add shapes for the ears.

## Step 2

Add lines for the pupils and sketch soft lines around the eyes. Add a line to the nose. Sketch in the shapes for the open mouth and add lines for the cheek. Starting with the front left leg, sketch the outline. Add lines for the front right leg. Using the ellipses as a guide, add the remaining lines for the rear leg and bottom. Lightly sketch lines for the tail and add shapes for the paws and the sharp claws. Sketch in some of the background and begin to build detail in the mane.

# Step 3

Erase any unnecessary lines. With a sharp pencil, refine the outline of the entire drawing, varying its pressure and the line style as you go. Keep your pencil moving freely when working on the mane to help create long, curved lines. When refining the eyes, press heavily and take care with the pupils. Add teeth and shade inside the mouth. Add soft contour lines to the face to create volume and to show the direction of the fur on the head. Add contour lines to the mane, legs and tail and add more details to the rock and horizon.

*Leave some areas white*

*Leave some areas white*

### DRAWING TIP

Dark fur can be created with layers of heavy, flat shading and loosely drawn contour lines. Leave highlights to show variety in the fur's texture.

# Step 4

Build the dark mane using layers of flat shading and loosely drawn contour lines. Leave some areas white (or light gray) to add texture. Add flat shading to parts of the legs and head and to the rock. Darken the claws, eyes, nose and mouth. Draw whiskers and spots along the upper lip and add more contour lines and shading to the head and nose. Leave the chin, cheeks and patches near the eyes white.

**INTERESTING FACT** → Lion cubs are born blind. They open their eyes about two weeks after birth but their eyes don't function properly for about another week.

# PIRANHA

*This South American freshwater fish has razor-sharp triangular teeth and a protruding lower jaw (like a bulldog), which are perfectly suited to stripping meat from bones. Piranha gather in schools, not just as a means of attack, but also as a defense against their natural predators: river dolphins and alligators.*

## Before you begin

The key element of this drawing is the fierce expression on the faces of both fish, combined with their razor-sharp teeth. The shapes of each fish are simple, so spend time on steps 3 and 4 creating the details of their eyes and mouths.

## Step ①

Holding your pencil loosely, lightly sketch the large circular shape for the forward-facing piranha. Add further lines for the tail and body. Sketch an outline for the jaw and add a circle for the eye. Draw the main ellipse for the other piranha. Add an ellipse for the head and circles for the eyes. Sketch lines for the open mouth and a shape for the tail.

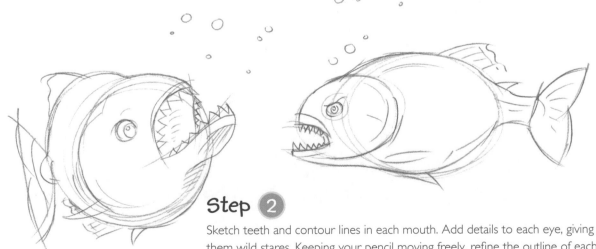

## Step ②

Sketch teeth and contour lines in each mouth. Add details to each eye, giving them wild stares. Keeping your pencil moving freely, refine the outline of each body. Add fins and other contour lines and small circles for bubbles.

## Step ③

Erase any unnecessary lines and soften any rough line work. With a sharp pencil, refine the overall outline, smoothing the curved lines of the bodies as you go. Add black areas to each pupil (leaving white highlights) and refine the sharp teeth. Add more contour lines to each body. Begin to create the effect of water by using loose, flat shading in the background.

### DRAWING TIP

To give an object volume, shade close to the outline, but leave a small gap along the edge. This creates a highlight, which stops a drawing looking flat.

Add shading to show deep-set eyes

Leave highlights

Add highlights

## Step ④

Darken the outlines. Use a combination of flat shading, contour lines and wriggly line work to build shadow areas and an underwater effect. Leave highlights along the outline of each piranha's body and add scales and texture to their skin. Leave the inside of the bubbles white. Use your eraser to add highlights across the whole drawing.

INTERESTING FACT → Despite their vicious reputation, piranha are typically not aggressive, with some kept as pets in home aquariums.

cool things to draw: deadly Animals

# POLAR BEAR

*Adult male polar bears weigh around 1100 pounds and measure nearly 10 feet from nose to tail. Large feet with pads covered in papillae (like tiny suction cups) and short, stocky claws mean polar bears can use sea ice as a platform for hunting their main source of food: seals.*

## Before you begin

The main element of this drawing is the contrast between the simple shapes of the bear and the small amount of shadow used. This helps create the effect of being in the Arctic. The nose, eyes and claws should be the darkest areas of this drawing.

## Step

Using a clock-face to check the angle, rule the main guidelines. Lightly sketch in the head ellipse and circles for the ears, nose and mouth. Add smaller circles for the eyes and lines for the nose. Draw four ellipses for the feet. Sketch the main lines of each front leg and the back leg.

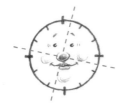

## Step 2

Keep drawing lightly. Sketch a large curved line for the back and bottom. Add a curve for the big belly and lines for the rear legs. Draw the remaining lines for the shoulders and the foremost leg. Sketch in the paw and claw details. Erase some of the lines around the nose and add details to the snout and ears. Sketch in soft line work for the pack ice.

# Step ③

Soften or erase any unnecessary lines. With a sharp pencil, refine the overall outline, smoothing the large curves as you go. Add some furry edges to the outline of the legs. Darken the eyes, leaving small highlights in each one. Refine the facial features and add flat shading under the chin and to the partly hidden rear leg. Add soft contour lines to create volume and texture. Sketch in a gentle shadow and add tone to some of the ice.

## DRAWING TIP

To give the effect of bright light, ice or snow, use small areas of shadow and leave lots of white space.

*Use soft shading technique*

# Step ④

With a sharp pencil, darken the outlines and refine the drawing. Using a light touch, add contour lines and shading to some areas. Leave most of the drawing white. When adding the furry contour lines, press lightly. Add soft, flat shading to the ocean and build some shadows in the ice pack.

*Leave most areas white*

## INTERESTING FACT ➔ Polar bears may have evolved from a population of brown bears that became isolated some 200 000 years ago when glaciers covered much of Eurasia.

# PYTHON

*Pythons are found throughout Africa, Asia and Australia. Most species have heat-sensing organs, enabling them to hunt in total darkness. They are non-venomous and are renowned for their sheer size, with the world's longest recorded snake measuring almost 33 feet.*

## Before you begin

The main feature of this drawing is the use of curves and shading. Having a loose grip on your pencil will help you draw smoother curves.

## Step

Using a clock-face and ruler, draw the main guideline. Align the following set of ellipses along this line. Drawing freely and pressing lightly, sketch the head ellipse. Add one ellipse for the eye and one for the snout. Below this, and touching the guideline, sketch a large ellipse. Add another large ellipse for the snake's neck and the small ellipse at its center. Sketch the remaining two ellipses, using your thumb and a pencil to measure distances. Add the final long, curved line.

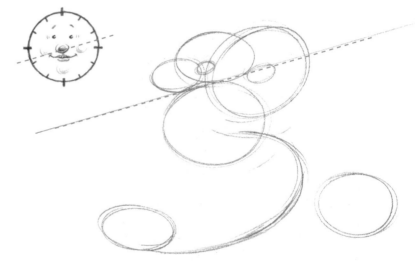

## Step 2

Sketching lightly, add a forked tongue and a tiny triangle for the open mouth. Sketch a vertical slit in the eyes and begin to add scales on the forehead. Refine the outline of the head. Look at the S-shape made by the snake's body below the head and sketch in the remaining curves. Draw the other curved lines for the rest of the body. Add a second S-shaped curve on the belly to mark where the belly ends and the back begins. Refine the outline and add detail to the background.

# Step ③

Erase any unnecessary lines. With a sharp pencil, refine the line work of the head and the outline of each curved body shape, varying the pressure to create depth: the closer the body part is, the darker the line work needs to be. Use a sharp pencil to add details to the eyes. Add a fine line for the mouth and darken the tongue. Using a soft touch, sketch the belly pattern and add the snake-skin pattern to the rest of the body. Use flat shading and contour lines to begin to add depth and tone.

## DRAWING TIP

Create depth in a drawing by softening the line work in areas that are further away.

Add a fine dark line for the mouth

# Step ④

Build the snake-skin effect using flat shading and contour lines within each scale section. Use a sharp pencil to refine the scale outlines, especially on the snake's head and neck. Leave a highlight along the top edge of each scale. Add soft contour lines to the belly, leaving much of it white, and dark contour line work and flat shading to the darker areas of the body. Leave highlights along most of the outlines to create volume. Add shadows to the ground and rocks and tone to the background.

Leave highlights

Leave a gap

Leave highlights

INTERESTING FACT → Being non-venomous, pythons kill by wrapping their body in coils around their prey and squeezing until it stops breathing. The python then swallows the prey whole.

# GREAT WHITE SHARK

*Typically weighing in at around one ton and measuring around 16 feet, the great white (also known as the white pointer) cruises the coastal waters of the world's major oceans. It eats mainly fish, dolphins, porpoises and seals. A big meal can satisfy a great white shark for up to two months.*

## Before you begin

The main feature of this drawing is the impressive torpedo shape of the shark's body and the way it appears to be leaping from the water. The overall outline is simple, so much of the drawing's strength comes from the detail in that massive jaw.

## Step 1

Using a clock-face and ruler, lightly sketch the main guideline and the horizon line. Sketch short lines for the top and bottom of the jaw and add two long, curved lines for the body. Sketch the curves for each fin and the ellipse and other shapes for the fish.

## Step 2

Lightly sketch lines for the lower half of the shark's body, including the tail fin. Add five lines for the gills. Sketch the curved outline of the jaws and the lines of razor-sharp teeth. Add shapes for the eye and brow. Refine the curved tip of the snout and the lines of the mouth. Add contour lines to the body, details to the fish and waves to the ocean. Sketch in a few clouds.

## Step ③

Erase the ruled guideline and any other unnecessary lines. With a sharp pencil, refine the smooth outline of the body, fins and tail. Darken the eye and refine the line work of the jaws and teeth. Add contour lines and shading to the inside of the mouth and cross-hatching and flat shading to the dark areas of the skin. Leave highlights along the edges of the fins and body to show volume and shine. Add more soft watery splash shapes to show movement. Sketch water droplets and details on the fish.

## Step ④

Build the dark areas of the shark's skin using layers of flat shading and contour lines. Leave highlights along the gills and the edges of main body parts. Leave the belly mostly white, but add some flat shading and cross-hatching to show volume. Using a heavy pencil line, go over the outline one more time. Darken the eye, but leave a small highlight inside it. Darken the inside of the mouth, especially towards the back. Use flat shading on the ocean and softer contour lines for the sky. Add shading to the fish, leaving some highlights. Add tone and watery line work over the shark's tail fin, and then erase parts of it to create the effect of splashing water.

*Build heavy layers of flat shading and contour lines*

*Leave highlights*

*Use a strong dark outline*

**INTERESTING FACT** ➡ Great white sharks do not chew their food. Powerful jaws and rows of serrated, razor-sharp teeth rip prey into pieces, which can then be swallowed whole.

# TARANTULA

*Tarantulas are large, hairy, carnivorous spiders that feed on insects, lizards, mice and birds. Tarantulas grab their prey, inject it with paralyzing venom, crush its body, shower it with digestive enzymes to liquefy it and then suck the result into their straw–like mouth opening. While many people have a fear of tarantulas, this spider is harmless to humans.*

## Before you begin

The main feature of this drawing is the hairy effect shown on the spider's body. There are no straight lines here, and only a few smooth curves. Keep your line work scratchy!

## Step 1

Using a clock-face and a ruler, sketch two guidelines. Drawing lightly, add the four main ellipses for the body and the eight smaller ellipses for the feet.

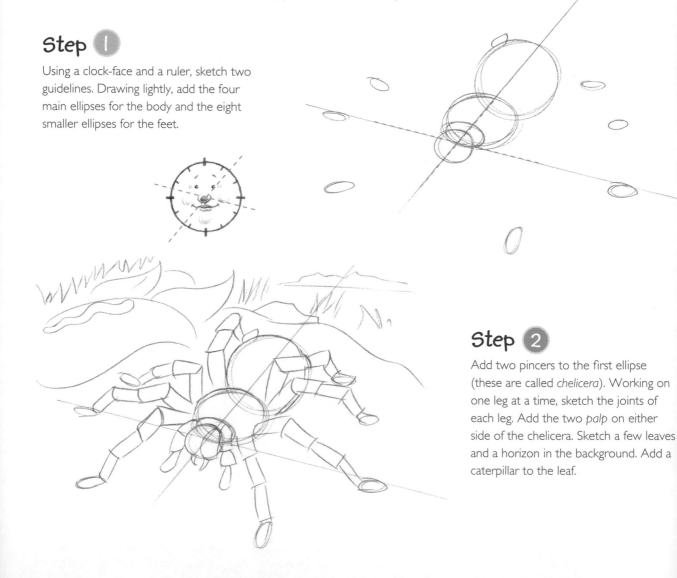

## Step 2

Add two pincers to the first ellipse (these are called *chelicera*). Working on one leg at a time, sketch the joints of each leg. Add the two *palp* on either side of the chelicera. Sketch a few leaves and a horizon in the background. Add a caterpillar to the leaf.

# Step ③

Erase the guidelines. Using a quick scratchy technique, add hairs to every section of the legs, body, chelicera and palp. Begin to add contour lines to every second section of the legs to create the striped effect. Add tiny circles to the *cephalothorax* (its eyes). Draw contour lines and a hairy outline to the *abdomen* and small shapes (*spinnerets*) near the bottom.

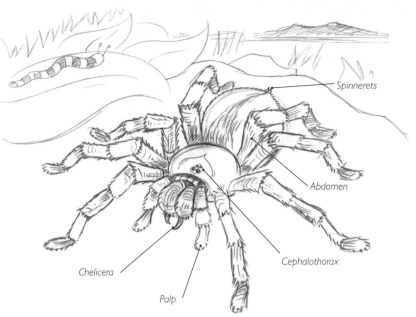

Spinnerets

Abdomen

Cephalothorax

Chelicera

Palp

# Step ④

Use lots of scratchy flat-shading to build tone, especially in the black sections of each leg and on the chelicera. Using a sharp pencil, darken the eyes and the area around the palp and chelicera. Add dark, scratchy hair lines over the entire body and a soft shadow below the tarantula. Leave a highlight on the abdomen and cephalothorax and along the edges of each leg. Add tone and detail to the background.

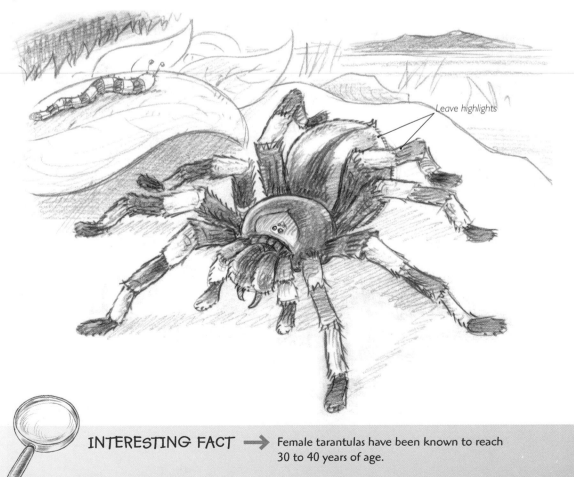

Leave highlights

INTERESTING FACT → Female tarantulas have been known to reach 30 to 40 years of age.

116

# TIGER

*Tigers can grow up to 13 feet long and weigh about 660 pounds. At the top of their food chain, these big cats fear no predator. Tigers hunt alone. Over short distances, they can reach speeds of up to 40mph. After bringing their prey to the ground, tigers kill instantly with a bite to the neck or throat.*

## Before you begin

The major elements of this drawing are the detail on the head and the striking pattern of the tiger's coat. Use lots of flat shading and contour lines in step 4. Build the drawing's structure carefully so you can decorate the final stage with lots of detail.

## Step

Using a ruler and a clock-face, lightly sketch the three main guidelines. Holding your pencil loosely, sketch the main head circle. Add ear shapes and ellipses for the nose and jaw and two small circles for eyes. Using your thumb and a pencil to plot distances, sketch the main ellipse for the rear leg. Add six small ellipses for the feet and legs, one for the shoulder and a circle for the curl of the tail.

## Step 2

Sketching lightly, add pupils and other lines around the eyes. Draw the nose tip and the line work around it. Add teeth and lines for the jaw, detail the ears and refine the outline of the head. Sketch in lines for the front legs, one at a time, using the ellipses to guide you. Add the lines of the belly and lines for the rear legs. Draw claws and toes on each paw and sketch in the bottom and the lines for the tail. Add the line work for the back and some contour lines to the body and legs. Lightly sketch in some background detail and a baseline.

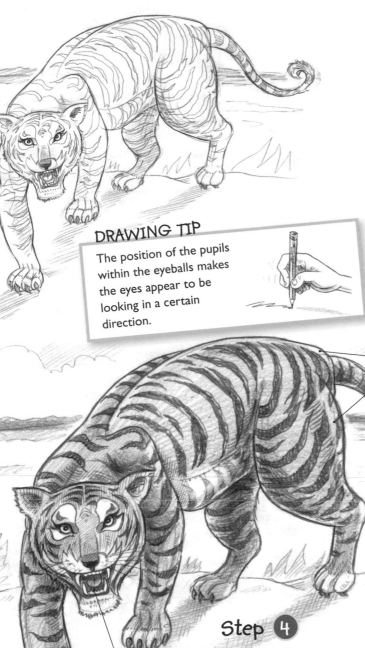

## Step ③

Erase or soften any unnecessary line[ Sharpen your pencil and refine the outline of the entire drawing, adding some furry texture to the tail and ears. Give the tiger sharp claws and strong muscles. Darken the eyes and their outlines, sharpen the teeth and add definition to the shape of the head. Add contour lines to the rear leg, the shadow on the ground, the ears, nose and mouth and the horizon. Lightly sketch each tiger stripe outline.

### DRAWING TIP

The position of the pupils within the eyeballs makes the eyes appear to be looking in a certain direction.

*Leave highlights*

## Step ④

Use layers of flat shading and contour lines to build tone in the coat. Leave some areas lighter than others and leave highlights along the outline of each body part to add volume. Leave the belly and toes white. Add flat shading to the darker areas of the legs and head and the rock. Darken the claws, eyes, nose and mouth and add soft shadows to the eyes. Add whiskers and spots along the upper lip and more contour lines and shading to the head and nose. Leave the chin, cheeks and patches near the eyes white. Add tone to the stripes, pressing heavily in dark areas while leaving some parts of some of the stripes a light gray to add volume. Add some clouds and tone to the sky and ground.

*Use a variety of shading and pencil marks to build detail*

### INTERESTING FACT ➜ Tigers can leap as high as 16 feet and as far as 30 or 35 feet in a single bound.

# WOLF

*The wolf is the largest wild member of the **Canidae** family, which includes dogs, foxes, dingoes and coyotes. An ice age survivor originating around 300 000 years ago, wolves are highly adaptable and have thrived in forests, deserts, mountains and urban areas. Wolves have strong social instincts and complex facial and body language. Their howl is used to communicate with other wolves.*

## Before you begin

The key elements of this drawing are the strong shape made by the wolf's body and the expression on its face. Once again, spend time detailing the eyes and mouth and the result will impress!

## Step 1

Sketch the main guidelines using a ruler and a clock-face. Position the other shapes around these lines using your thumb and a pencil to plot distances. Noticing how they overlap or touch the guidelines, sketch ellipses for the head, rear leg and feet. Sketch in lines for the neck and back and ellipses for the eyes and nose. Add lines for the ears and snout.

## Step 2

Add details to each eye. Add soft lines around the eyes, tone to the nose and lines for the mouth. Create some furry edges on the head's outline and detail the ears. Add lines for the first front leg and paw. Sketch in the other front leg and paw and the rear legs. Add curves for the tail. Refine the shape of the neck, shoulder and back and add lines for the belly. Sketch in some background and add the beginnings of the furry coat.

## Step ③

Erase any unnecessary lines. With a sharp pencil, refine the outline of the head, paying attention to the snarling shape of the mouth and teeth. Add very dark outlines to the eyes and leave white highlights within each pupil. Use a scratchy, firm line to refine the body shape, noticing how most of the fur is drawn in short- to medium-length strokes. Add contour lines to the shaded legs, the ground and the background. Use soft shading on the fur to build tone and variety in the fur. Add contour lines to the head and neck.

## Step ④

Use layers of flat shading and scratchy contour lines to build the fur coat. Leave many areas white and some gray. Vary the pressure with your pencil to add texture. Create an overall shade in the background, leaving a slight gap around the wolf's outline. Add further shading to the ground. Refine the snarl and nose. Add tone to the head, leaving gaps of white around the eyes, mouth and ears. Sketch contour lines to show the direction of the fur.

*Flat shading and scratchy contour lines add texture*

*Leave white*

*Leave white*

INTERESTING FACT  During winter months, wolves can travel over 30 miles per day in search of food.

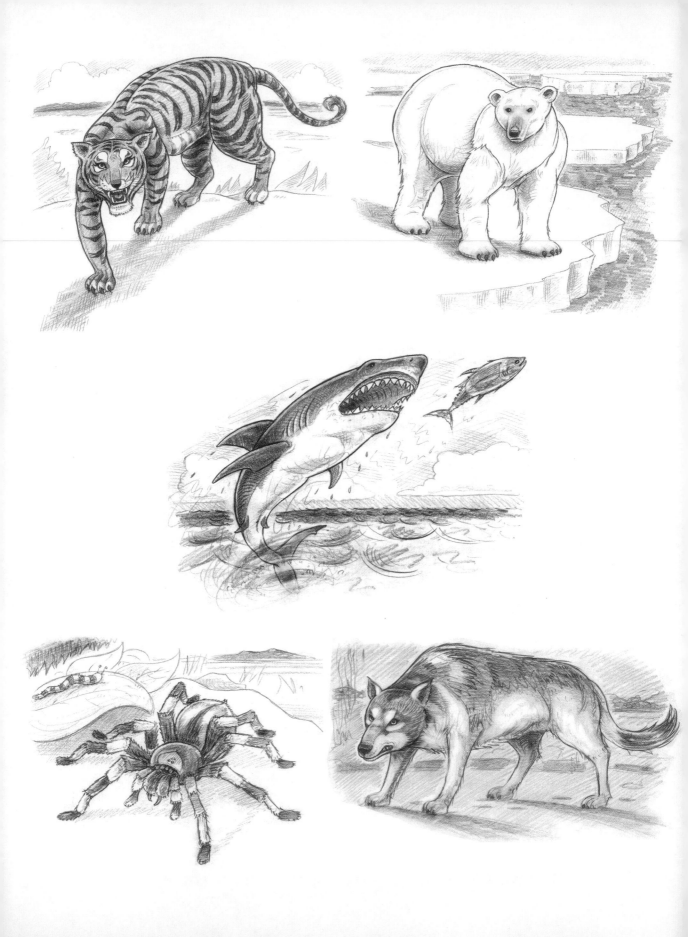

# Cool
# Things to Draw
# Space

shane Nagle

# Cool things to Draw

# Space

© GALACTIC II

# INTRODUCTION

*The beauty and mystery of the night sky has fascinated humankind for thousands of years. It has taught us about our place in the universe and inspired us to voyage into space in search of other forms of life.*

*Learn how to draw some of the creatures you might meet on your space travels and the exciting ships you could encounter out in deep space!*

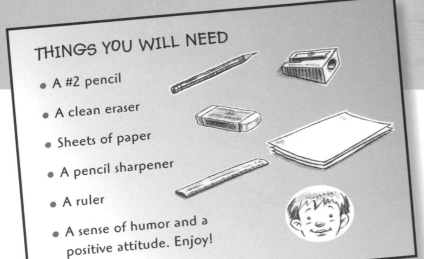

## THINGS YOU WILL NEED

- A #2 pencil
- A clean eraser
- Sheets of paper
- A pencil sharpener
- A ruler
- A sense of humor and a positive attitude. Enjoy!

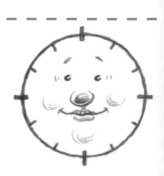

## Using the clock-face

This fun tip will help you sketch lines at different angles.
*Look at the line you want to draw.*
*Now imagine that line on a clock-face: where would it point?*
*Draw a line on your page, matching the angle on the imaginary clock-face.*

## Drawing guidelines

When drawing your space voyage, pay attention to these things:

1 Each drawing begins with basic shapes and guidelines
2 Always draw lightly at first
3 Focus on one part of the drawing at a time
4 Build texture and volume in layers
5 Experiment with different pencil techniques as you go along
6 Practice, practice, practice!

# Step-by-step drawing

Each drawing is made by following steps. Read through all the steps carefully before you begin, then follow them one at a time until your drawing is done. Don't worry if your drawing looks different to the examples; all artists find their own style and your skills will improve with practice.

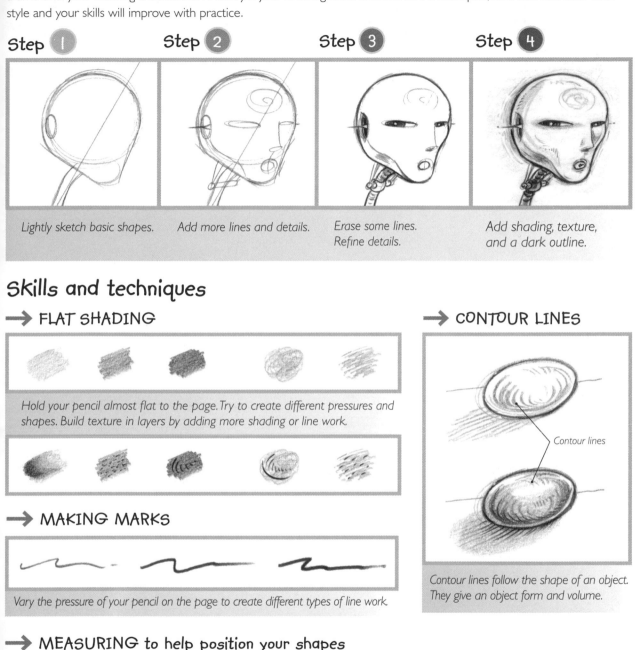

Step 1 — Lightly sketch basic shapes.

Step 2 — Add more lines and details.

Step 3 — Erase some lines. Refine details.

Step 4 — Add shading, texture, and a dark outline.

# Skills and techniques

## → FLAT SHADING

Hold your pencil almost flat to the page. Try to create different pressures and shapes. Build texture in layers by adding more shading or line work.

## → CONTOUR LINES

Contour lines

Contour lines follow the shape of an object. They give an object form and volume.

## → MAKING MARKS

Vary the pressure of your pencil on the page to create different types of line work.

## → MEASURING to help position your shapes

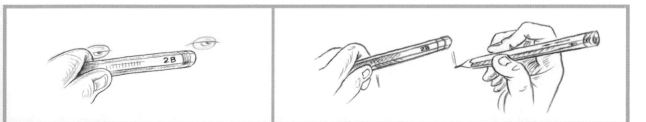

Use a pencil like a ruler, marking the distance with your thumb. Mark that length with another pencil on your paper.

# GRAY ALIEN

*Gray aliens are the most common, stereotypical image of an extraterrestrial. They feature in many movies, television programs, and books about aliens and are often associated with stories of alien abductions.*

## Before you begin

The most important elements of this drawing are the unusual body proportions: a large head and very thin limbs. Long, flowing lines help capture the lightness in its step. Don't worry about being too exact.

## Step 1

Sketching lightly, draw an ellipse for the head and some jaw lines. Sketch a curved line for the spine, a shoulder line, and two shoulder ellipses. Add small ellipses for the waist, knees, and feet. Sketch lines for the upper legs, using a clock-face to check the angles. Draw the baseline and horizon lines.

## Step 2

Add curves to the face and two lines for the neck. Sketch a hand shape, two thin ellipses for muscles, and lines to create the long, thin raised arm. Repeat this with the lower arm. Add torso lines, flowing them into the lines of the upper legs. Sketch the tapering lines of the lower legs. Add the feet and a UFO in the background.

## Step ③

Erase or soften the ellipses and structural lines within the body outline. Add details to the hands and feet. Begin to refine the outline with a sharp pencil. Erase some of the head ellipse and then darken the eyes and facial features, leaving white highlights in the eyes. With a soft pencil, add texture to the skin. Perhaps your gray's skin is translucent, so you can see some of its internal organs. Add contour lines to UFO to make it look like it is spinning.

## Step ④

Using a sharp pencil, create a strong outline. Create volume with contour lines and a small amount of shading and add more details to the skin texture. Using a variety of flat shading styles, such as cross-hatching and squiggly lines, build layers of night sky. Refine the UFO's outline with a sharp pencil and add a shadow beneath it.

**INTERESTING FACT** ➡️ Grays are portrayed as about four feet tall with gray skin, slanted oval eyes, long arms, and a small thin body. Even in the late 19th century, writers such as H.G. Wells were writing about such creatures.

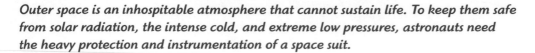

cool Things To Draw: space

# ASTRONAUT

*Outer space is an inhospitable atmosphere that cannot sustain life. To keep them safe from solar radiation, the intense cold, and extreme low pressures, astronauts need the heavy protection and instrumentation of a space suit.*

## Before you begin

This drawing is made from a basic structure based on simple shapes and lines. The details in the face, helmet, and the space suit material will help make the drawing look realistic.

## Step 1

Sketch the main guideline using a ruler and a clock-face. This line is used to position all the shapes. Add different-sized circles for the helmet and shoulders. Sketch the light on the helmet, the torso, and the waist lines. Add ellipses for the knees and boots, and lines for the upper legs.

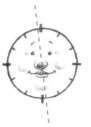

### DRAWING TIP

To create the appearance of glass, use an eraser to soften details and add highlights.

## Step 2

Add the outline of the lowered arm, curved lines for the elbow, and shapes for the wrist and glove. Repeat this for the outstretched arm. Add lines for the chest panel and the remaining lines for the legs. Sketch the outlines of the boots. Add guidelines for the face and further lines to the helmet.

# Step ③

Erase any unnecessary lines. Working on one element at a time, detail the space suit outline with a sharp pencil. Add folds in the material and sketch knee pads and the shoulder logo. Add details such as straps, tubes, pockets, patterns, and patches. Refine the fingers and the glove outlines. Add a thick heel and sole and other details to the boots. Refine the facial features with a sharp pencil. Leave a gap around the inside circle of the helmet, and begin to add shading and other details. Lightly sketch in a backpack and begin to sketch the background.

# Step ④

Darken the details using a heavy, sharp line and build volume and texture in layers. Use flat shading, cross-hatching, contour lines, and different pencil marks and pressures to create a variety of details on the space suit and its components. Imagine the sun is casting a shadow and leaving highlights. Leave a gap around the lowered arm to make it stand out from the suit. Build the shading and details of the helmet and use an eraser to add highlights and soften the facial details. Add cross-hatching and shading to the background, leaving a gap along the edge of the drawing.

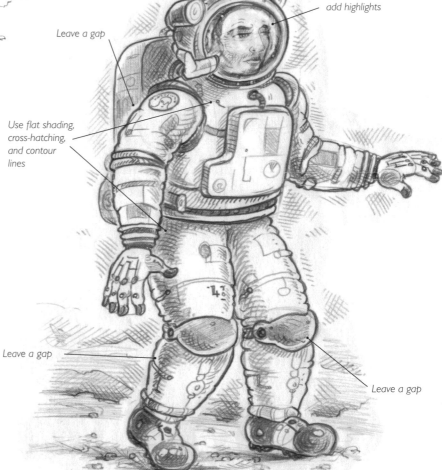

Use an eraser to soften details and add highlights

Leave a gap

Use flat shading, cross-hatching, and contour lines

Leave a gap

Leave a gap

**INTERESTING FACT** → Because sound is caused by vibrations in the air, if someone shouted in your ear while you were out in the airlessness of space, you wouldn't hear them.

# EARTH POD

*One day, public transport in space may look something like this pod. Smaller than a space shuttle and more like a school bus, Earth pods travel between lunar stations and across short distances in space.*

## Before you begin

The key element to this drawing is its smoothly curved form. Another element which gives the drawing atmosphere is the layers of shading used for outer space. Leaving areas of white behind each pod helps create a sense that they are moving.

### DRAWING TIP

To make it seem as though an object is moving, use an eraser to soften lines and shading.

## Step ①

Work on the largest pod first. Lightly sketch a large ellipse and add the wing lines. Sketch a c-shaped line for the nose cone and add the front window line. Now repeat this for the two smaller pods.

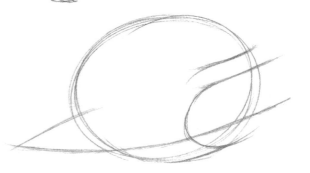

## Step ②

Erase some of the ellipse where it crosses under the wing. Add a curved line to show where the wing attaches to the pod's body. Erase any unnecessary lines on the nose cone and complete its shape, drawing lightly. Finish the front window shape and add ellipses along the side. Add two jet exhaust shapes to the rear, the antenna, some contour lines, and details to the body.

## Step ③

Erase any unnecessary lines and soften any patchy line work. Refine the overall shapes and the outline with a sharp pencil, smoothing the curves as you go. Begin to add soft contour lines. Refine the details of the windows, wing tips, jet exhaust, and nose cone.

*Use an eraser to soften lines and shading to add movement*

*Use an eraser to soften lines and shading to add movement*

## Step ④

Darken the outlines and other details with a sharp pencil. Make the surface look smooth and shiny with layers of flat-shading and contour lines. Build darker layers of shading and contour lines on the belly and nose cone. Add details for the interior, the logos, and a shaded panel down the side. Leave highlights on the windows and along the edge of the shaded areas to add volume and shine. Use flat shading and other textures to create the space background. Leave a lighter highlighted area around each pod to help it stand out. Leave the area behind each pod white and add movement lines using the side of a pencil.

*Use an eraser to soften lines and shading to add movement*

**INTERESTING FACT** ➡️ Our solar system's gravitation fields, magnetic fields, solar winds, and solar radiation could one day be used as propulsion methods for space travel.

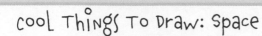

# FIGHTER RAY

*The galactic police force, which is charged with protecting humankind, patrols the galaxy in fighter rays such as these. Equipped with lasers and electromagnetic shields, these slick vehicles travel at four times the speed of sound!*

## Before you begin

Only a few straight lines are used here. Observe the curved shapes and the outline and remember to loosely hold your pencil when sketching the initial shapes and lines.

## Step 1

Sketch the main "spine" guideline using a ruler and a clock-face. Use this line to position the other shapes. Sketching lightly, work on the largest fighter first. Draw a long curved line crossing the spine guideline. Add a triangular shape to each end of the curved line. Sketch small ellipses and circles along the spine and the nose curve. Add the two outlines of the smaller fighters.

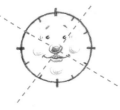

## Step 2

Using smooth lines, connect the triangular wing tips to the nose curve. Add details to the nose area, including two small lasers. Add shapes for the jet exhausts and a teardrop shape that starts on the tail and ends behind the nose. Sketch more tail details, and add the pilot and the interior inside the forward ellipse. Add details to the smaller fighters.

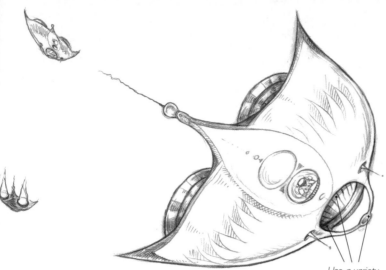

## Step ③

Erase any unnecessary lines and soften any patchy line work. Refine the overall shapes and outline with a sharp pencil, smoothing the curves as you go. Add shading to the nose area and the jet exhausts. Refine the details of the lasers, pilot, windows, and wing tips. With a sharp pencil, lightly sketch a pattern on the wings. Begin to add shading and contour lines. Shade the body of the smallest fighter, leaving the jet trails white.

*Use a variety of shading*

## Step ④

Darken the outlines and refine the details. Make the paintwork interesting using layers of flat-shading and contour lines. Darken the wing tips, tail, and exhausts. Leave highlights on the windows and along the edge of shaded areas. Using the side of your pencil, softly draw jet streams and smoke rings. Add cross-hatching and flat shading and sketch some curly lines to show air currents.

*Use patches of cross-hatching*

*Leave jet streams white*

*Leave highlights*

INTERESTING FACT ➡ These nimble fighter rays are designed to resemble a manta ray as it glides effortlessly through the oceans.

# GALACTIC STARSHIP

*This enormous starship can travel huge distances between the civilizations and planets of the galaxy. The crew may spend most of their lives living and working on the ships, which are so large that they are like small cities.*

## Before you begin

This drawing is based around a large elliptical shape. The remaining elements are attached to it. Spend time observing and measuring this ellipse. Movement lines and white space behind the starship give the appearance of speed.

## Step 1

Drawing lightly and using a clock-face create the correct angle, sketch the main ellipses, making sure they overlap each other. Add a line for the tail fin and sketch the smaller ellipses and the other lines.

*The two ellipses overlap here*

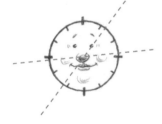

## Step 2

Lightly add lines to complete the tail fin and sketch shapes for each jet exhaust. Complete the engine on the underside and add a long window shape. Begin to mark out tiny windows and the logo. Add some contour lines and details to the body.

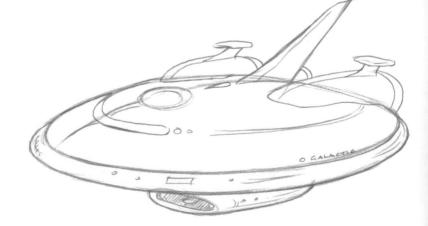

# Step ③

Erase any unnecessary lines and soften any rough line work. With a sharp pencil, refine the overall outline, smoothing the curved lines as you go. Begin to add soft contour lines to the windows, engine, exhausts, and tail fin. Add more tiny windows and body details.

### DRAWING TIP

Correction fluid can be used to add lights, windows, and stars to dark areas.

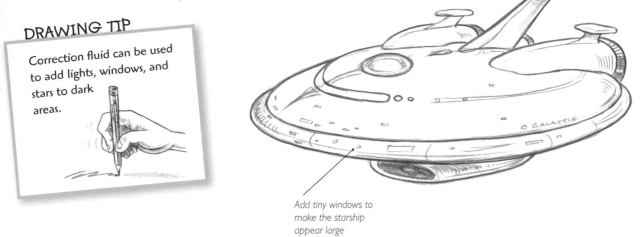

Add tiny windows to make the starship appear large

# Step ④

Leave some of the tiny windows white. Use layers of flat shading and heavy contour lines on the rim, exhaust tips, tail fin, and engine. Add details and shading to the large glass dome and the long window area. Leave highlights on the windows and along the edge of the shaded areas to add volume and shine. Darken the outlines with a sharp pencil and add other details. Build layers of flat-shading and contour lines along the tail and the exhaust areas. Use flat shading and other textures to create the space background. Leave the area behind the starship white and add movement lines using the side of your pencil.

Use an eraser to soften lines and to create a movement effect

Leave a gap

Leave a gray highlight

**INTERESTING FACT** ➡ To reduce the use of fossil fuels, vehicles will be powered by non-chemical methods, like the electromagnetic propulsion system of this galactic starship.

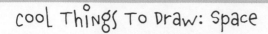 cool Things To Draw: Space

# GALACTIC STATION

*Traveling between stars requires complex space stations. Designed to independently sustain human, alien, plant, and animal life for long periods in space, they transport equipment and supplies, and provide for scientific as well as social needs.*

## Before you begin

The main element of this drawing involves the ellipses, circles, and other shapes along the spine. Take care with the positioning of the ellipses for the nose section, as the perspective in this drawing owes a lot to getting this part right.

*Observe how the ellipses sit close together on this side*

## Step 1

Using a clock-face to check the angle, rule the main spine line. Use this line to position the other shapes. Sketch the two large ellipses of nose section, making sure one sits close to the edge of the other. Add the smaller ellipse, placing it close to the left side of the large ellipses. Add the remaining ellipses and lines to the spine and two floating circles. Sketch the outline of a fighter ray on the lower circle.

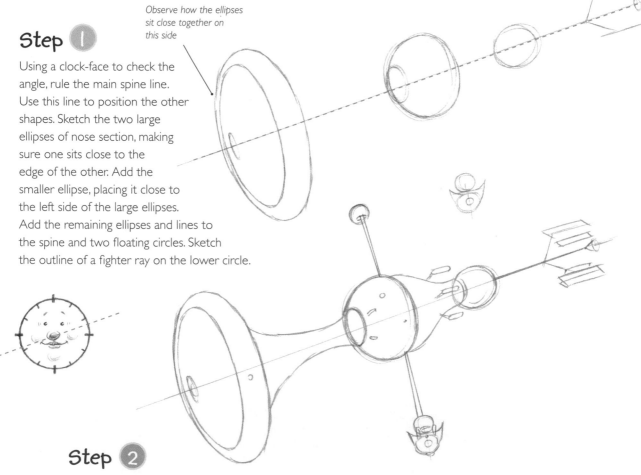

## Step 2

Drawing lightly, add lines to complete the neck section. Notice how smoothly these lines attach to the central section. Sketch the remaining shape of the central section and add rectangular shapes for the solar panels. Refine the tail. Use a ruler to add lines for the steel bridges. Refine and add other details to the body.

## Step 3

Erase the spine guideline, soften any rough line work, and remove any unnecessary lines. With a sharp pencil, refine the overall outline, smoothing the curved lines as you go. Begin to add soft contour lines to the body sections, leaving a gap along each edge to show volume. Add details to the solar panels and steel bridges. Sketch some tiny fighter rays and their movement lines. Add tiny windows over the station.

### DRAWING TIP

Leaving a gap along the edge of shaded parts creates volume.

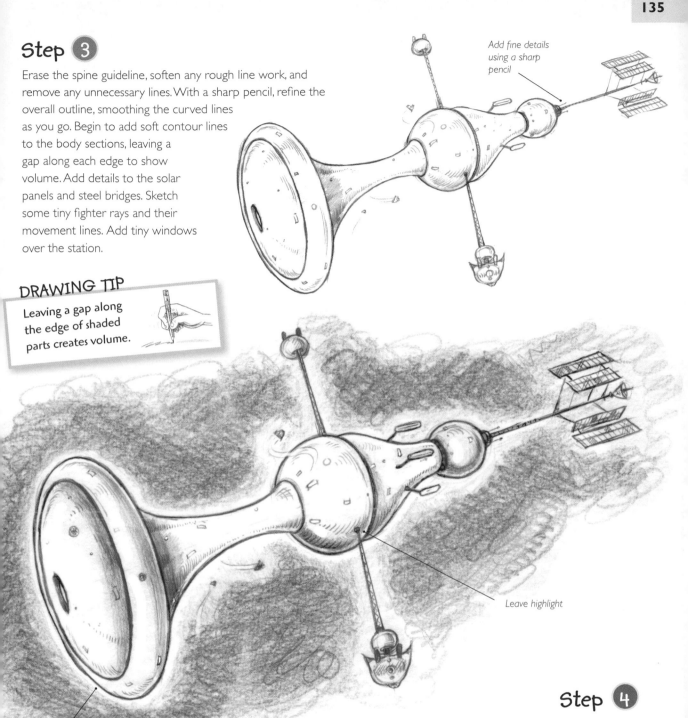

Add fine details using a sharp pencil

Leave highlight

Leave a gap

## Step 4

With a sharp pencil, darken the outlines and refine other details. Use flat shading and contour lines to build volume, leaving a gap along each edge. Leave some of the tiny windows white. Create the effect of outer space using layers of flat-shading and other marks. Leave a space around the space station so it stands out. After shading the background, if you have correction fluid, add dots of white for stars.

INTERESTING FACT → Building space stations requires the cooperation of thousands of highly skilled people from different civilizations.

# HELP-BOT

*It is likely that the development of robots will continue to advance. If so, most homes might one day have their own help-bot for cooking, house cleaning, and even home schooling and child-minding needs.*

## Before you begin

Apart from the three basic sections used in the initial steps, the key element of this drawing is the details used on the more intricate body parts, such as the arms and neck. Enjoy contrasting the dark areas with the lightly shaded body parts.

## Step ①

Sketch the main guideline using a ruler and a clock-face. Use this line to position the other shapes. Add a circle and lines for the head and the ear ellipse. Drawing lightly, add two s-shaped lines for the neck. Sketch a small ellipse at the base of these lines. Add the horizontal shoulder line and a curved line running from the small neck ellipse down along the spine line. Add the torso shape, shoulder ellipses, and the wheel circle.

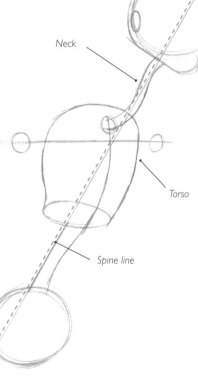

Neck

Torso

Spine line

Leg

## Step ②

Working on one section at a time, add ellipses for the facial features and guidelines to the head. Sketch neck bolts and add antennas to ears and the back. Draw the shoulder shapes and the torso details. Lightly sketch the steel leg and add a mudguard and axle shapes to the wheel section. Sketch the elbow and hand shapes, and add thin lines for the metal arms.

# Step ③

Erase any unnecessary lines. With a sharp pencil, refine the outline of the head and the facial features. Define the neck and bolts and add contour lines. Darken the neck hole and refine the torso outline. Add details to the arms and hands, and to the rubber shoulder components. Refine the leg shapes and mudguard, and add tread lines to the wheel. With a light pencil, sketch a futuristic cityscape in the background.

# Step ④

Using heavy, sharp line work, darken the components and outlines. Use flat shading, contour lines, and different pencil marks and pressures to show variety in the components. Imagine the sun is casting a shadow and shade this in on the ground behind the bot. Use heavy shading and gray highlights to show the spinning black wheel. Darken the rubber shoulder components, the elbows, and the neck. Add shading to the ground and the cityscape.

*Shadow cast by the neck*

*Use heavy flat shading, contour lines, and highlights*

INTERESTING FACT ➜ Robots are regularly used in factories to make items such as cars and machinery. Doctors use robots to perform surgery. One robot of the future may be as small as a molecule.

# PLANETS

*Planets can be either terrestrial, which means they are made of rock, like the Earth, or gas giants, which are usually massive balls of gaseous material. Planets are large enough to create their own gravitation pull. This means they have an atmosphere, as their gravity keeps gas particles close to their surfaces.*

## Before you begin

The main element of this drawing is a shaded sphere: the planet Saturn. Observe a ball in the sun to help draw this, paying attention to any highlights along the circumference. Notice how the shadow area of a sphere is on the opposite side to where the light is coming from. Use a highlight of gray around the overall sphere to set it apart from the background.

## Step 1

Drawing lightly and holding your pencil loosely, sketch a large circle for Saturn. Add long thin ellipses for its dust rings. Sketch circles for the remaining planets and their moons.

## Step 2

Before erasing any line work, refine the circles and ellipses with a sharp pencil. Add other rings around Saturn and create contour lines on these rings. Imagine the Sun shining down from the upper right hand side of the page. Use soft contour lines to begin shading each planet and moon.

# Step ③

Erase any unnecessary lines. With a sharp pencil, refine and smooth the outlines of each circle and ellipse. Use flat shading to build the main shadow areas of each sphere and then use a variety of line work, pencil pressures, and cross-hatching to add texture and volume. Shade some of the rings, while leaving others white. Leave highlights around the perimeter of each sphere.

*Use a variety of shading and line work*

*Saturn casts a shadow on its rings*

*Shade some of the rings*

*Build layers of flat shading and cross-hatching*

## DRAWING TIP

Always have a gentle pencil grip when sketching guidelines for circles and ellipses.

# Step ④

Use layers of flat shading and lots of cross-hatching to build the outer space background. Leave gaps around each sphere so they stand out. Build more layers of shading and contour lines on each planet and moon, giving each planet a slightly different texture. Finally, darken the outlines again.

*Leave highlights*

**INTERESTING FACT** → The solar system consists of the Sun, eight planets, at least three dwarf planets (called Ceres, Pluto, and Eris), more than 130 satellites or moons, and a large number of small bodies, like comets and asteroids.

cool Things To Draw: space

# SPACE STATION

*The International Space Station is an orbiting research station. The ISS is due for completion after 2010 and will have involved the cooperation of 16 countries. Estimates of the cost to build the International Space Station range between $92 and $130 billion dollars.*

## Before you begin

Examine the structure of this drawing. It is built in two parts, each using simple guidelines and shapes. Spend time getting the initial stages right and the rest of the drawing will be much easier. Use your thumb and a pencil to plot distances.

## Step 1

Using a ruler and a clock-face, draw the guidelines for the shuttle and the International Space Station (ISS). Sketch a curved line for the Earth. Add a small ellipse for the nose cone tip, an s-shaped curve behind the cockpit, and then the rest of the nose cone. Sketch ellipses and lines for the module. Add the curved wing line, and lines for the tail fin, cargo bay, and the UFO.

Module

Nose cone

Cockpit

## Step 2

Sketch the cargo bay door. Add lines for the wing, tail fin, and exhausts. Sketch the windows and add contour lines to the nose cone. Add more details to the module, the telescopic arm, and an astronaut. Using a ruler, add structural lines to the ISS, including solar panels at each end and the spine of modules.

Spine of modules

Astronaut

Telescopic arm

# Step 3

Erase any unnecessary lines. Using a dark outline, refine the shapes of the shuttle with a sharp pencil. Using softer line work, but still with a sharp pencil, refine the details of the ISS. Leave a gap around the shuttle wing to separate it from the ISS drawing. Begin to add cross-hatching and contour lines to all elements.

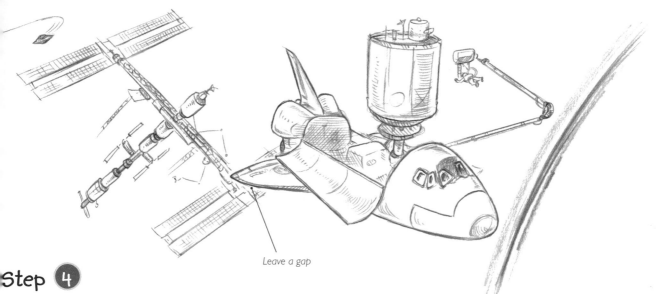

*Leave a gap*

# Step 4

Refine your drawing further, building dark layers of flat-shading and heavy contour lines on the nose cone. Add flat shading and soft contour lines to the cargo bay door, fuselage, module, and tail fin. Leave highlights on the windows and along the edge of the underbelly and nose cone. Use layers of flat shading and contour marks to build the space background. Leave a gap around the Earth's curve and around each component. Add details to the Earth's surface using layers of shading and other markings. Create stars using correction fluid.

*Leave a gap*

**INTERESTING FACT** ⟶ The ISS has meant that space tourism has become a reality, with people paying huge amounts of money to visit it. The ISS experiences 16 sunrises and sunsets a day as it orbits.

cool Things To Draw: space

# UFOS

*UFOs (unidentified flying objects) and flying saucers have been reported for centuries, but the twentieth century saw an increase in reports. Many sightings are actually weather balloons, aircraft, astronomical occurrences, or clouds, but many are also unable to be explained.*

## Before you begin

The main elements in this drawing are the long curved lines. Hold your pencil loosely and sketch lightly using long strokes. Don't worry about making mistakes. It's all part of the fun!

## Step 1

Work on the large UFO first. Drawing lightly and holding your pencil gently, sketch the two ellipses. Add curved lines for the rim and underbelly. Repeat this method for the smaller UFOs.

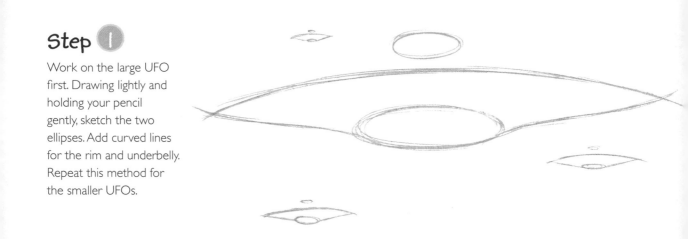

## Step 2

Again, begin with the largest UFO. Erase the bottom part of the upper ellipse and sketch curves for the upper half of the body. Add contour lines to the entire object. Repeat this method for each UFO.

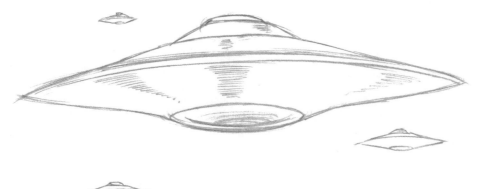

# Step 3

Erase or soften any unnecessary lines.
With a sharp pencil, refine the overall
outlines and smooth the curved lines.
Create a shiny metallic effect using
contour lines, leaving highlights
along all shaded edges.
Add soft lines to create
a spinning motion.

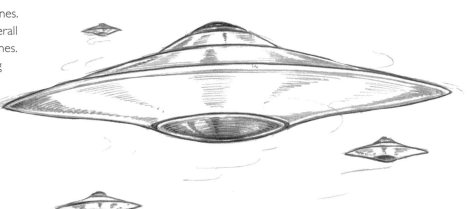

# Step 4

Darken the outlines of the main UFO. Add soft, flat shading to most of the body
areas, leaving some sections white to create the spinning effect. Sketch in clouds
using the side of a pencil. Add flat shading around the clouds and use cross-
hatching to build texture. Use an eraser to add movement lines.

*Use an eraser to add
movement lines*

INTERESTING FACT → Perhaps the earliest depiction of UFOs are rock carvings of cylindrical
objects resembling spacecraft on an island in Hunan Province, China.
They are thought to be approximately 47 000 years old.

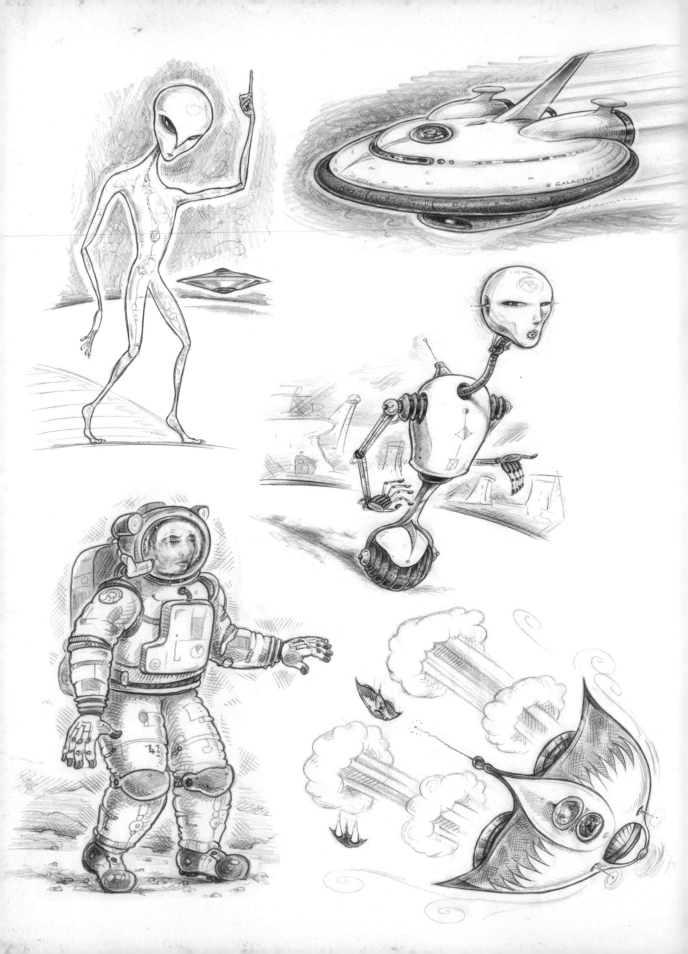

# Cool
# things to Draw
# Speed
# Machines

Shane Nagle

# Cool things to Draw

# Speed Machines

# INTRODUCTION

Something inspires humans to move faster than our legs can carry us. Perhaps it is the breathtaking speed of a cheetah, the swiftness of gliding dolphins in the sea or the sight of a shooting star. Whatever the reason, we have built machines that can carry us at extraordinary speeds across the land, sea and sky.

Inside these pages are some of the fastest machines on the planet. Pick the ones that inspire you the most and discover how easy they are to draw!

## THINGS YOU WILL NEED

- A #2 pencil
- A clean eraser
- Sheets of paper
- A pencil sharpener
- A ruler
- A sense of humor and a positive attitude. Enjoy!

## Drawing guidelines

When drawing your speed machines, pay attention to these things:

1 Each drawing begins with basic shapes and guidelines
2 Always draw lightly at first
3 Focus on one part of the drawing at a time
4 Build texture and volume in layers
5 Experiment with different pencil techniques as you go along
6 Practice, practice, practice!

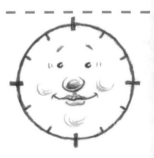

## Using Clock-face

This fun tip will help you sketch lines at different angles.

Look at the line you want to draw.

Now imagine that line on a clock-face: where would it point?

Draw a line on your page, matching the angle on the imaginary clock-face.

# Step-by-step drawing

Each drawing is made by following steps. Read through all the steps carefully before you begin, then follow them one at a time until your drawing is done. Don't worry if your drawing looks different to the examples; all artists find their own style and your skills will improve with practice.

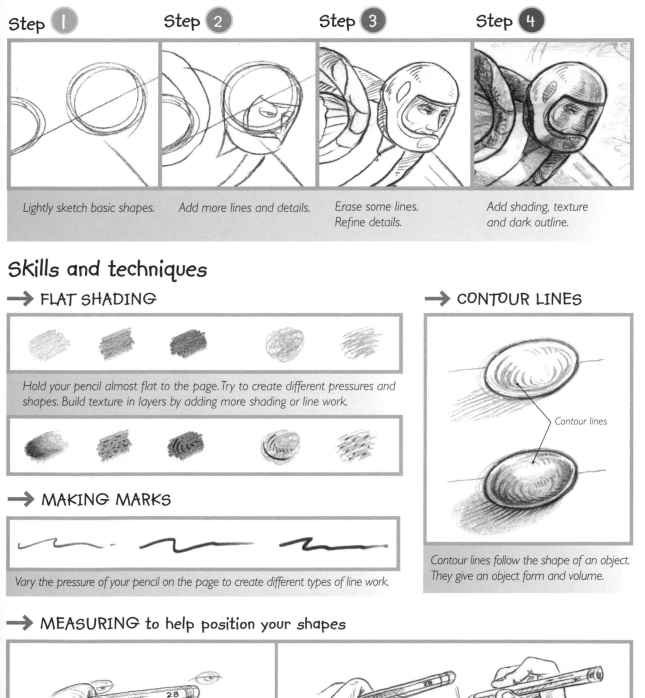

**Step** 1

**Step** 2

**Step** 3

**Step** 4

Lightly sketch basic shapes.

Add more lines and details.

Erase some lines. Refine details.

Add shading, texture and dark outline.

# Skills and techniques

→ **FLAT SHADING**

Hold your pencil almost flat to the page. Try to create different pressures and shapes. Build texture in layers by adding more shading or line work.

→ **MAKING MARKS**

Vary the pressure of your pencil on the page to create different types of line work.

→ **CONTOUR LINES**

Contour lines

Contour lines follow the shape of an object. They give an object form and volume.

→ **MEASURING** to help position your shapes

Use a pencil like a ruler, marking the distance with your thumb. Mark that length with another pencil on your paper.

# BLACKBIRD SR-71

*From its creation in 1964 until its retirement in 1998, the Blackbird SR-71 remained the world's fastest (and highest-flying) piloted aircraft. On July 28 1976, an SR-71 broke the world speed record for its class by reaching 2193mph.*

## Before you begin

The most important element in this drawing is the striking shape of the SR-71. Take your time to plot the angles and curves in steps 1 and 2, and don't forget to always draw lightly at first.

## Step 1

Using a ruler and a clock-face, sketch in guidelines A and B. Use your thumb and a pencil to plot the position of the *nose tip* and wing tips and then sketch in lines for each wing.

## Step 2

Sketch in the line work for the *fuselage* and the *tail*. Add shapes for the cockpit windows and curves to each wing tip. Lightly add circles for each jet engine and then sketch in lines for the engines and their tail fins. Add details to the engines and shapes for the tail. Add the sharp *spike* at the front of the plane.

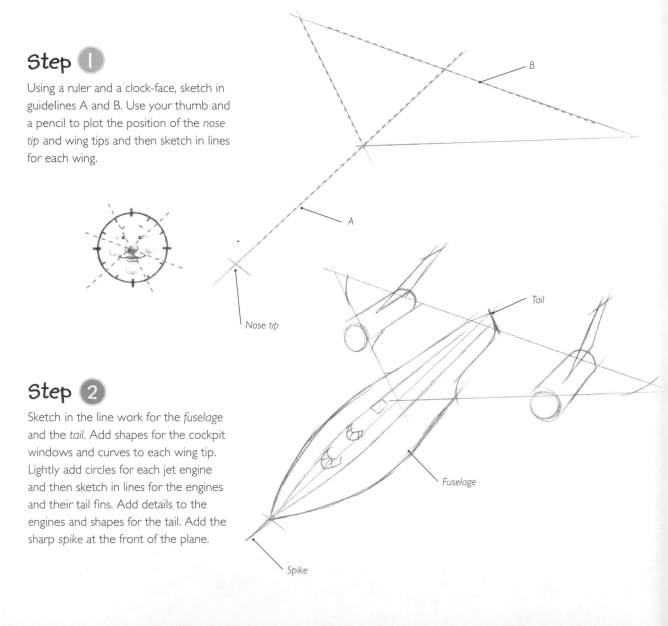

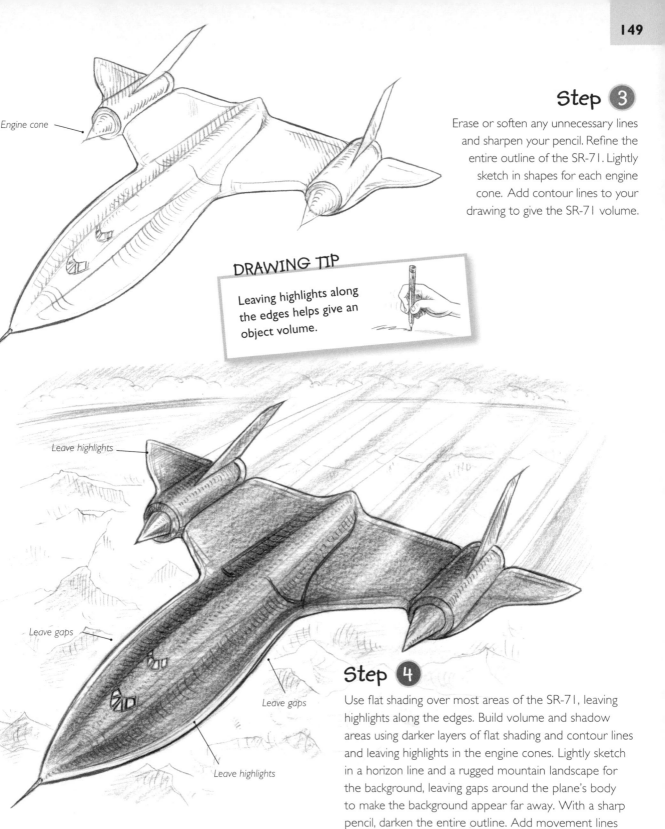

Engine cone

## Step 3

Erase or soften any unnecessary lines and sharpen your pencil. Refine the entire outline of the SR-71. Lightly sketch in shapes for each engine cone. Add contour lines to your drawing to give the SR-71 volume.

### DRAWING TIP

Leaving highlights along the edges helps give an object volume.

Leave highlights

Leave gaps

Leave gaps

Leave highlights

Leave highlights

## Step 4

Use flat shading over most areas of the SR-71, leaving highlights along the edges. Build volume and shadow areas using darker layers of flat shading and contour lines and leaving highlights in the engine cones. Lightly sketch in a horizon line and a rugged mountain landscape for the background, leaving gaps around the plane's body to make the background appear far away. With a sharp pencil, darken the entire outline. Add movement lines using flat shading and an eraser.

INTERESTING FACT → The SR-71 could photograph a car's license plate from an altitude of 80 000ft.

cool things to draw: speed machines

# BOBSLEIGH

*Bobsleighs are sleek, gravity-powered sleds. Bobsleighing is a popular winter sport, with crews of two or four people racing down narrow, twisting, banked ice runs. These sleighs are capable of reaching speeds of up to 80mph.*

## Before you begin

The main element of this drawing is its use of curved lines. Keep your arm loose as you lightly sketch them in.

## Step 1

Using a clock-face and a ruler, sketch the long guideline for the blades. Add a shorter second ruled guideline for the blades on the other side, ensuring it is at a different angle to the first. Drawing lightly, sketch two long curved lines for the bobsleigh's body and add a curve for the *front wing*. Sketch an ellipse for the helmet and lines for the rear of the sled. Lightly sketch in long curves for the track.

Front wing

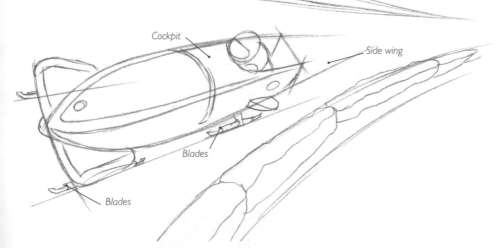

Cockpit

Side wing

Blades

Blades

## Step 2

Still drawing lightly, sketch in the rest of the front wing. Add more contour lines to the *cockpit* and the bobsleigh's body, including the small *side wing* and the badges. Add ellipses and other shapes for the first and second driver. Add the *blades* using a sharp pencil. Lightly sketch more line work for the track.

## Step ③

Erase or soften any unnecessary lines. Sharpen your pencil and refine all the outlines and details. Darken the blades using a sharp pencil. Add softer contour lines and begin to build shadow areas. Lightly sketch in a background.

### DRAWING TIP

To make an object appear to be moving quickly, create movement lines with an eraser.

Use an eraser to create movement lines

## Step ④

Build shadow areas using layers of flat shading, cross-hatching and contour lines. Add contour lines to the track, leaving highlights to create volume. Add facial features to the driver and decorative shapes to both helmets. With a sharp pencil, darken the outlines and other details such as the helmet, wings and blades. Add further soft details to the background and the track.

INTERESTING FACT → The bobsleigh is named for the way crews "bob" back and forth to increase their speed.

cool Things To Draw: speed machines

# FORMULA ONE

*Formula One (F1) is the highest class of car racing in the world. Devised and governed by the FIA (Fédération Internationale de l'Automobile), it had its first season in 1950. Over time, the sport's enormous popularity and budgets has led to the development of remarkably advanced machines, racing at speeds of up to 225mph.*

## Before you begin

The key features of this drawing are the shapes made by the large tires. Notice how most of the F1 car sits below the top of these tires. Use lots of flat shading and contour lines to create a rubbery effect.

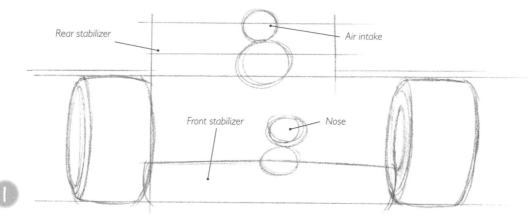

## Step ❶

Using a ruler, sketch in the baseline. Checking their height with your thumb and a pencil, sketch the second guideline for the top of the front tires and two shorter lines for the top of the rear tires. Lightly sketch in curved shapes for each front tire. Add ruled guidelines for the *rear stabilizer* and ellipses for the helmet, *air intake* and nose. Lightly sketch in the *front stabilizer*.

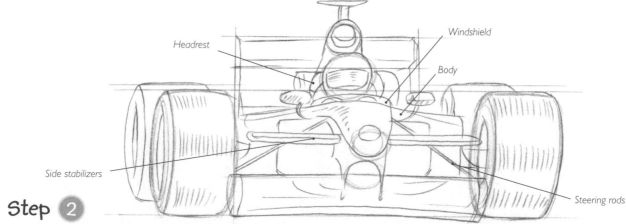

## Step ❷

Drawing lightly, sketch the *side stabilizers* and add further details to the front stabilizer. Detail the helmet, air intake and rear stabilizer. Add shapes for small mirrors and create the line work for the nose, the badge and the car's *body*. Sketch in two *steering rods* behind the side stabilizers. Add two rear tires, a *headrest* and a small *windshield*.

# Step ③

Erase or soften any unnecessary lines. Sharpen your pencil and darken the outline of the tires. Working on one part at a time, refine the outlines of the front and side stabilizers, the steering rods and the body and nose shapes. Define the mirrors, the windshield, the helmet, the headrest, the air intake and the rear stabilizer. Add soft contour lines to the tires and to other shadow areas. Lightly sketch in a background.

## DRAWING TIP

When drawing objects in the distance, use a softer pencil pressure.

# Step ④

Build the tires, the road surface and the shadow areas using layers of flat shading, contour lines and cross-hatching. Leave gaps around the edges of objects to help them stand out. Leave a shine on the windshield, the helmet and the front and rear stabilizers. Add further contour lines to each section to help create volume. With a sharp pencil, darken the outlines of each section of the car. Leave highlights on the tires so they appear to spin. Using a softer touch, add further details to the background.

Leave gaps

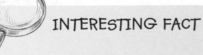

INTERESTING FACT → A modern F1 car has almost as much in common with a jet plane as it does with a road car. Aerodynamics play an important role in the sport, with race-car wings developed to increase speed and safety.

# JET-MAN

*Nicknamed "Jet-man", Yves Rossy is the first person to have successfully flown assisted by a jet engine–powered wing. After jumping from a support plane, Rossy unfolds the wing, starts the jet engines and flies. The wing then retracts and he returns to the ground with the aid of a parachute.*

## Before you begin

This drawing's main feature is the extraordinary spectacle of seeing a flying man! There is a fair bit of detail in Rossy's body shape and the jet engines, so take your time plotting these shapes in steps 1 and 2.

## Step 1

Using a clock-face and a ruler, sketch the three main guidelines. Starting with the head and shoulder, draw the ellipses and circles, plotting their location using your thumb and a pencil. Lightly sketch in lines for the front of the wing and the wing tips.

## Step 2

Sketch in lines for the helmet, neckline and facial features. Add lines for the arm and hand, a long shape for the chest and a line for the waist. Sketch in lines for the two *shoulder straps*. Starting at the waist, add lines for the *harness* and for each leg, knee and foot.

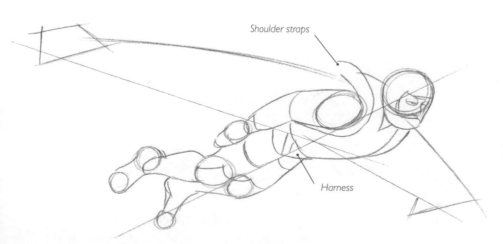

Shoulder straps

Harness

wing

## Step 3

Add shapes for the three jet engines and sketch in the second hand. Add the remaining structural lines to the *wing*.

## Step 4

Erase or soften any unnecessary lines and sharpen your pencil. Refine the helmet and face details, adding contour lines for shading and to create volume. Add details to the shoulder, arm and hand, and refine the shoulder straps and harness. Detail the knee pads and boots and then refine the outline of Rossy's whole body, including the second hand. Refine the jet engines and the wing shape, adding contour lines as you go.

## Step 5

Use a combination of flat shading and contour lines to build shadow areas and volume. Darken the waist harness, shoulder straps, *parachute*, knee pads and parts of each engine. Using a sharp pencil, refine the entire drawing. Leave shiny effects on the helmet and wing. Leave a gap around the main image and add a soft background of rivers, farms and roads, so it looks as though it is seen from above. Leave white space for the jet exhaust. Add movement lines, using an eraser to help.

*Parachute*

*Leave white space*

*Add movement lines*

 **INTERESTING FACT** → On the first successful flight in 2004, Rossy flew alongside his support plane for 4 minutes at a speed of 115mph.

156

# MAGLEV TRAIN

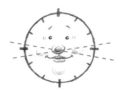

*Maglev (short for **magnetic levitation**) trains are high-speed passenger trains. They float over a guideway and use magnets instead of steel wheels on tracks like regular trains. Maglevs don't have engines as such: they use electromagnetic force as propulsion.*

## Before you begin

The main feature of this drawing is the use of perspective. Perspective is an effect that gives depth to a drawing by making long objects appear to be getting smaller as the distance increases. The main lines of the train are angled towards a distant vanishing point.

*Vanishing point*

A

B

## Step 1

Make a dot on the left side of your page. This is your *vanishing point*. Using a clock-face to check angles and your thumb and a pencil to check positions, rule guidelines A and B, making them intersect at the vanishing point. Rule the other two long guidelines. Add the shorter ruled lines for the front of the Maglev and one at the side for its door. With a light touch, sketch in the curved line at the front.

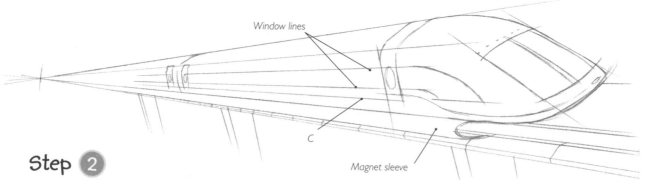

*Window lines*

C

*Magnet sleeve*

## Step 2

For the remainder of this drawing, all horizontal lines will be directed towards the vanishing point. Use your ruler to sketch the two *window lines* and then the line for the bottom of the *magnet sleeve*. Add line C, which runs between the magnet sleeve and the window lines. Add further lines for the concrete track, including the support poles. Drawing lightly, sketch the windows at the front of the train and the doors along the side. Draw ellipses for the small windows. Add curves at the front of the magnet sleeve (where it wraps around the track) and to the long side window.

# Step 3

Soften or erase any unnecessary lines, including the vanishing point. With a sharp pencil and ruler, refine the train's line work. Refine and smooth the curves at the front end of the train and darken all the remaining line work. Use contour lines to build darker areas and to show volume.

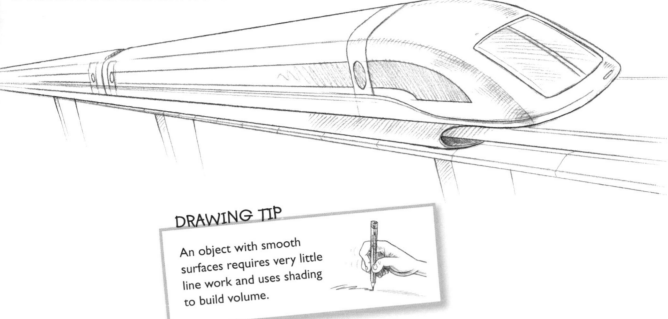

## DRAWING TIP

An object with smooth surfaces requires very little line work and uses shading to build volume.

# Step 4

Use flat shading and contour lines to build volume and to add shine to the train. Add dark layers of flat shading and contour lines to the windows and the magnet sleeve, leaving highlights along the edges. Sketch cross-hatching on the track's support poles and create shine effects on the windows using an eraser. Sketch in a soft background: a river below, a mountain to the left and a city to the right.

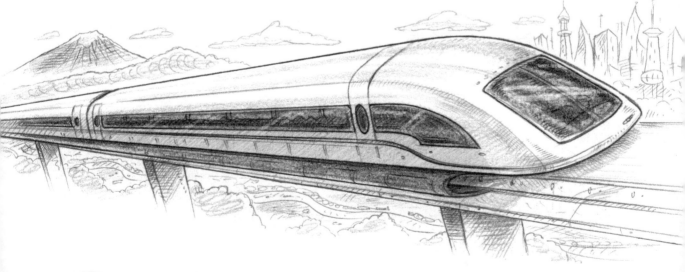

INTERESTING FACT → The highest recorded speed of a Maglev train is 361mph, achieved in Japan in 2003.

cool Things To Draw: speed machines

# SPACE SHUTTLE

*The space shuttle can orbit the Earth in roughly 90 minutes. When re-entering the Earth's atmosphere, its speed reaches an incredible 16 700mph, before it slows down to land at about 220mph.*

## Before you begin

The main feature of this drawing is the dramatic stream of hot gases made by the shuttle during re-entry. The contrast between this stream of mainly white space and the dark background allows the shuttle to be seen very clearly.

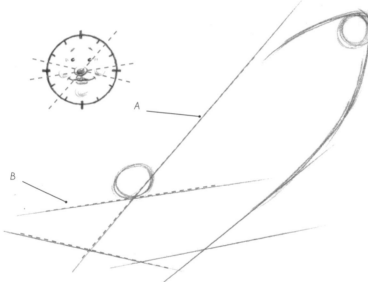

## Step ①

Using a ruler and a clock-face, sketch in guideline A. Add guideline B, ensuring that it is at a slightly different angle to A (to create the correct perspective). Rule in the remaining three guidelines for the wings using your thumb and a pencil to plot distances. Add the two circular shapes and lightly sketch the long curves for the fuselage and the nose cone.

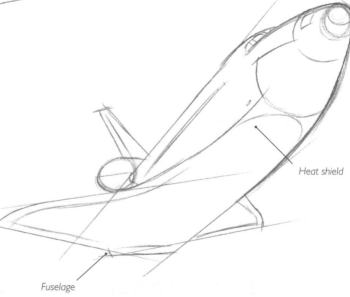

Heat shield

## Step ②

Add lines for the tail fin and sketch in the curve for the cockpit. Sketch in curved lines for each wing tip and add lines for the tail end of the *fuselage*. Starting at the left wing, lightly sketch in the line for the *heat shield*, noticing how it curves around the nose cone to help create volume. Still drawing lightly, add contour lines, windows and other details.

Fuselage

## DRAWING TIP

When building layers of flat shading for a night sky, use rapid movements with your hand and press heavily.

## Step 3

Erase or soften any unnecessary lines. Sharpen your pencil and refine the line work, smoothing the curves as you go. Begin to build shadow areas using cross-hatching and contour lines, leaving highlights along the edges. Lightly sketch in the curve of the Earth.

## Step 4

Use layers of heavy flat shading to build the night sky. Soften your pencil pressure around the edges and leave white space for the gas stream. Darken the entire heat shield with layers of flat shading and strong contour lines, leaving highlights to create volume. Darken the windows and leave highlights to create a glassy surface. Use flat shading and soft contour lines to give volume to other parts. Sketch in wriggly flat shading and other contour lines for the gas stream. Use an eraser to add movement lines to the image. Add stars with white paint or correction fluid, if available, and further details to the Earth.

*Leave white space*

*Leave white space*

INTERESTING FACT ➔ The shuttle's main engine weighs one-seventh as much as a train's engine, but it delivers as much horsepower as 39 locomotives.

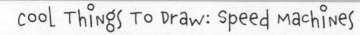

cool things to draw: speed machines

# SUZUKI HAYABUSA

*In the late 1990s, the Suzuki car company released the Hayabusa, a new breed of high-performance motorbike. "Hayabusa" is Japanese for "peregrine falcon". This extraordinary bird of prey is capable of exceeding speeds of 185mph, just like this amazing machine.*

## Before you begin

The main element of this drawing is its realism and detail. This is quite a complex image because very few geometric shapes are used to construct it. Take your time with steps 1, 2 and 3 and you will be speeding along in no time!

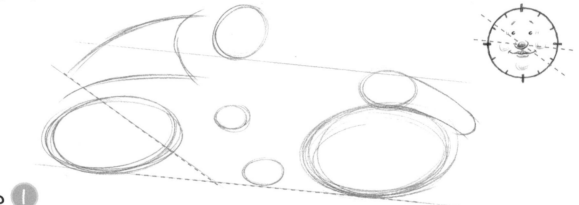

## Step 1

Using a clock-face and a ruler, sketch the baseline and its parallel guideline. Add the shorter ruled guideline. Using your thumb and a pencil to plot sizes and distances, loosely sketch the two wheel ellipses and the small ellipses between them. Add the shape over the rear wheel, the helmet ellipse and the shapes for the windshield.

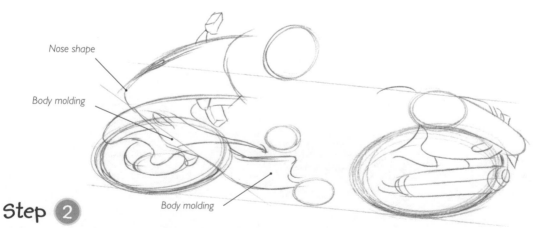

*Nose shape*

*Body molding*

*Body molding*

## Step 2

Lightly sketch in lines for the exhaust pipe, seat, tail lights and other details at the rear of the bike. Using the short, ruled guideline and the front ellipse to help you, sketch the curved line work of the *body molding*, including its *nose shape*. Sketch in the two small mirrors and front lights. Add the front mudguard and ellipses to the front wheel.

## Step ③

Add lines to the helmet visor and neck line. Sketch in ellipses for each hand and then add lines for both arms. Sketch in lines for the *fuel tank*. Lightly sketch in the rider's back and leg shapes, adding lines for the boot and pedal (near the exhaust pipe).

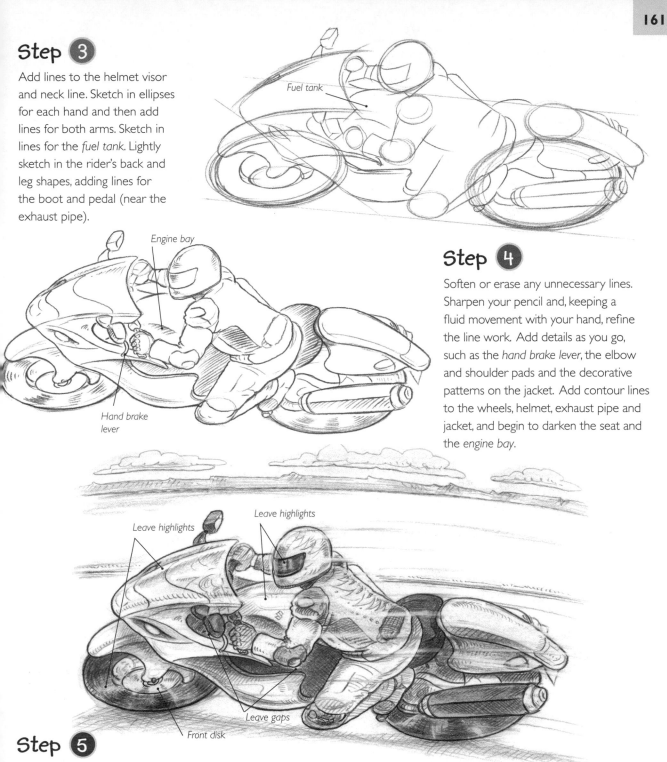

Fuel tank

Engine bay

Hand brake lever

## Step ④

Soften or erase any unnecessary lines. Sharpen your pencil and, keeping a fluid movement with your hand, refine the line work. Add details as you go, such as the *hand brake lever*, the elbow and shoulder pads and the decorative patterns on the jacket. Add contour lines to the wheels, helmet, exhaust pipe and jacket, and begin to darken the seat and the *engine bay*.

Leave highlights

Leave highlights

Leave gaps

Front disk

## Step ⑤

Use a variety of flat shading, cross-hatching and contour lines to create different surfaces, such as shoulder pads, shiny metal and dark spinning tires. With a sharp pencil, darken the outline, adding further details such as the helmet and the jacket design. Use darker layers of flat shading on the tires, engine bay, seat, mirrors and exhaust pipe. Add spinning contour lines to the *front disk* and to both wheels. Leave highlights to show volume. Add a shadow and a curved horizon. Create movement lines with an eraser.

**INTERESTING FACT** → The *Hayabusa* has a top speed of 208.5mph and can accelerate from 0 to 62mph in 2.77 seconds.

# ULTIMATE AERO

*The **Ultimate Aero** is the world's fastest production car, which means it is mass produced and street-legal, rather than a special-purpose vehicle like a Formula One car. The Aero holds the Guinness World Record for the fastest speed of 257mph.*

## Before you begin

The main element of this drawing is its use of curves. There are only a few geometric shapes to help construct it, so you will need to keep your hand moving freely to draw lots of curved line work.

## Step 1

Using a clock-face and a ruler, sketch in the baseline. Using your thumb and a pencil to check its position, add the parallel line. Lightly sketch ellipses for each wheel. Keeping a loose grip on your pencil, sketch line work for the side, front and back of the Aero.

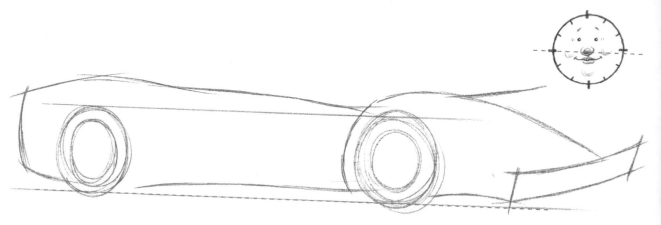

## Step 2

Still sketching lightly, add details to the wheels, making sure you add lines for each wheel bay (close to and around each wheel). Sketch in details such as the front lights, the molding along the side and front and the line for the door.

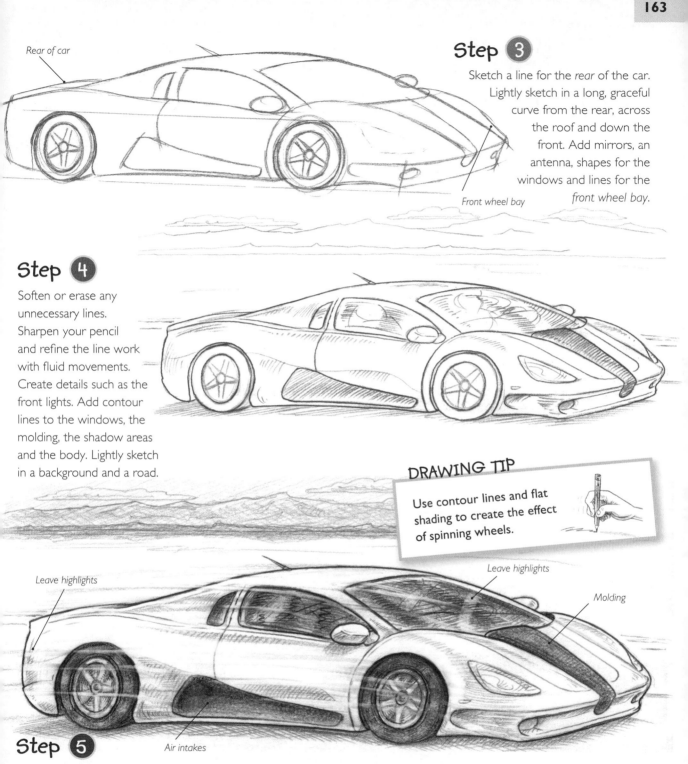

*Rear of car*

## Step ③

Sketch a line for the *rear* of the car. Lightly sketch in a long, graceful curve from the rear, across the roof and down the front. Add mirrors, an antenna, shapes for the windows and lines for the *front wheel bay*.

*Front wheel bay*

## Step ④

Soften or erase any unnecessary lines. Sharpen your pencil and refine the line work with fluid movements. Create details such as the front lights. Add contour lines to the windows, the molding, the shadow areas and the body. Lightly sketch in a background and a road.

### DRAWING TIP

Use contour lines and flat shading to create the effect of spinning wheels.

*Leave highlights*

*Leave highlights*

*Molding*

*Air intakes*

## Step ⑤

Add flat shading and contour lines to the wheels, leaving highlights to add texture and movement. Build dark layers of flat shading, pencil marks and contour lines on the tires, windows, *molding* and *air intakes*. Give the Aero smooth, flowing curves by adding flat shading and contour lines. Using a sharp pencil, refine the drawing's outlines. Add cross-hatching to the ground and further soft details to the background. Use an eraser and soft pencil work to add movement lines.

**INTERESTING FACT** → It took over seven years to design this limited-edition vehicle, which sells for well over $650 000.

cool Things To Draw: speed machines

# WESTLAND LYNX HELICOPTER

*At a European air show on August 6, 1986, a slightly modified Westland Lynx helicopter exceeded 249mph, making it the world's fastest helicopter. The Lynx is also an agile helicopter, capable of performing loops and rolls.*

## Before you begin

This drawing's main feature is the exciting rescue attempt it portrays. Lots of contour lines are used to create the effect of the spinning propeller blades, and the slight curve in the rescue cable and harness make it appear to be blown by the wind.

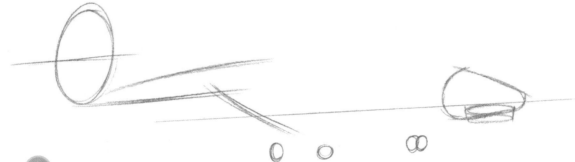

## Step 1

Drawing lightly, rule the main guideline, ensuring it is at a slight angle. Plotting their size and location using your thumb and a pencil, sketch the large ellipses for the tail propeller blade and the curves for the rear of the helicopter. Add the small wheel ellipses and shapes for the nose cone.

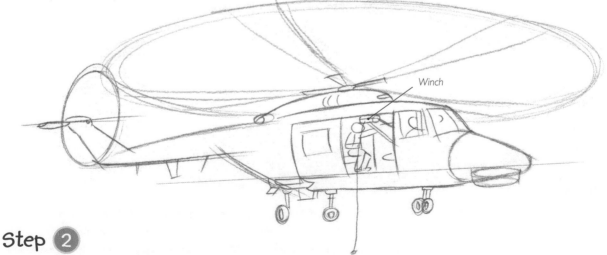

Winch

## Step 2

Still drawing lightly, add further lines for the tail section and sketch in the outline of the body. Add the door and window shapes and the undercarriage details. Sketch in remaining details, such as the figures inside the cabin, the *winch* and the rescue cable. Holding your pencil loosely, sketch the large ellipse and other lines for the main propellor.

## Step ③

Erase any unnecessary lines and soften any rough line work. With a sharp pencil, refine the helicopter's outline, smoothing the curves as you go. Add further details, such as the harness. Add contour lines for both propeller blades and create volume by adding contour lines and cross-hatching. Lightly sketch in the background, including the figure in the sea below.

## Step ④

Refine and darken the outlines and sharpen the details. Use a combination of flat shading, cross-hatching and contour lines to build shadow areas, especially in the cabin and on the nose cone. Build volume with layers of shading, leaving a shine on the nose cone and along the edges of the main body parts. Add waves to the ocean using rapidly drawn flat shading and line work. Create sunlight reflecting off the sea with an eraser and add further details to the background.

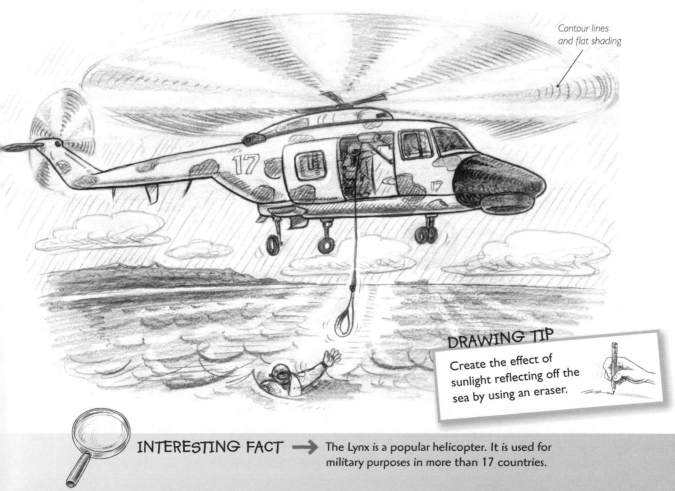

*Contour lines and flat shading*

### DRAWING TIP

Create the effect of sunlight reflecting off the sea by using an eraser.

**INTERESTING FACT** → The Lynx is a popular helicopter. It is used for military purposes in more than 17 countries.

# WIND-POWERED VEHICLE

*Land sailing involves moving across land in a wheeled vehicle fitted with a sail. The sail harnesses the power of the wind, propelling the vehicle forward. Historically used for fun, some enthusiasts today push the design of their wind-powered vehicles to increase their speed.*

## Before you begin

Examine the structure of this drawing. It has three main areas: (1) the mainly geometric shape of the sail, (2) the curved shapes of the body and (3) the background. Use your ruler to build and refine the sail and use your eraser to help add dust and movement lines.

### Step 1

Using a clock-face, rule the three main guidelines, noticing where they intersect each other. Plotting their size and position with your thumb and a pencil, add three ellipses for the wheels. Add the remaining line work of the sail and the shape for the tail of the body.

A

### Step 2

Lightly add more guidelines for the sail, including line A and the flag design. Drawing lightly, add the long curved shapes of the body and each wheel cover. Lightly sketch in the cloudy horizon.

## Step 3

Soften or erase any unnecessary lines and sharpen your pencil. Add wheel curves at the bottom of both visible wheel covers and then refine the details and outlines of the main body shape. Refine the curved line work at the front of the sail and define its remaining outline with a ruler. Softly add contour lines to the body and a logo on the front wheel cover.

## Step 4

Use flat shading, cross-hatching and contour lines to darken the paintwork and the flag pattern to build volume. Add a shadow on the ground. Leave highlights in the cockpit glass and along most edges. Softly add further details to the sky and sketch movement lines using a pencil held flat to the page. Use an eraser to create the effect of sand clouds on the body and movement lines on the sail.

*Erase small areas*

*Erase small areas*

**INTERESTING FACT** → A British project called *Windjet* (our drawing) is attempting to break the current wind-powered, land-speed record of 116.7mph.

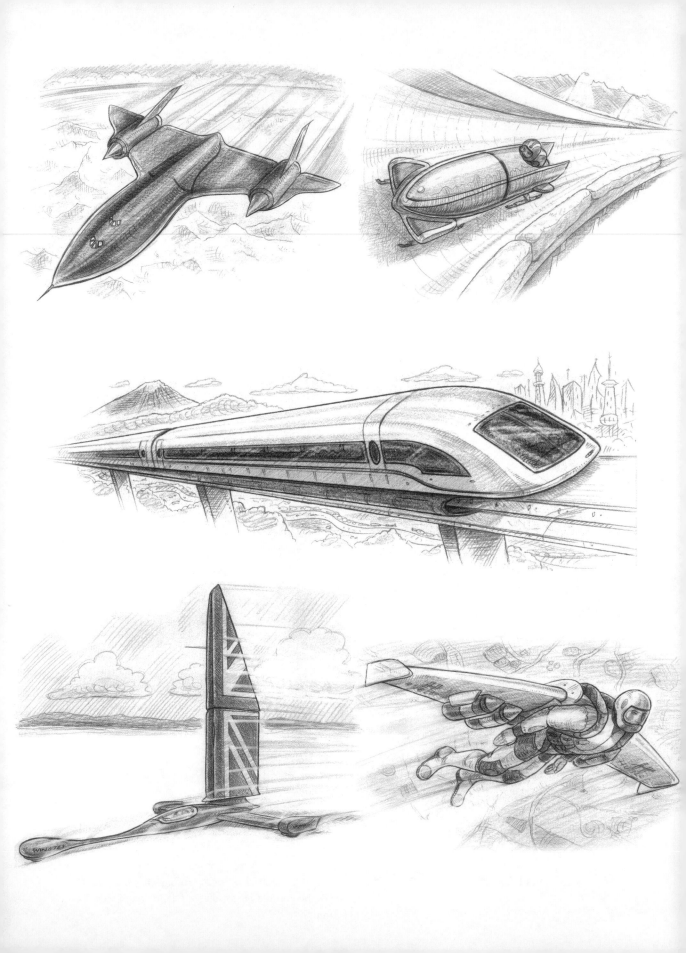

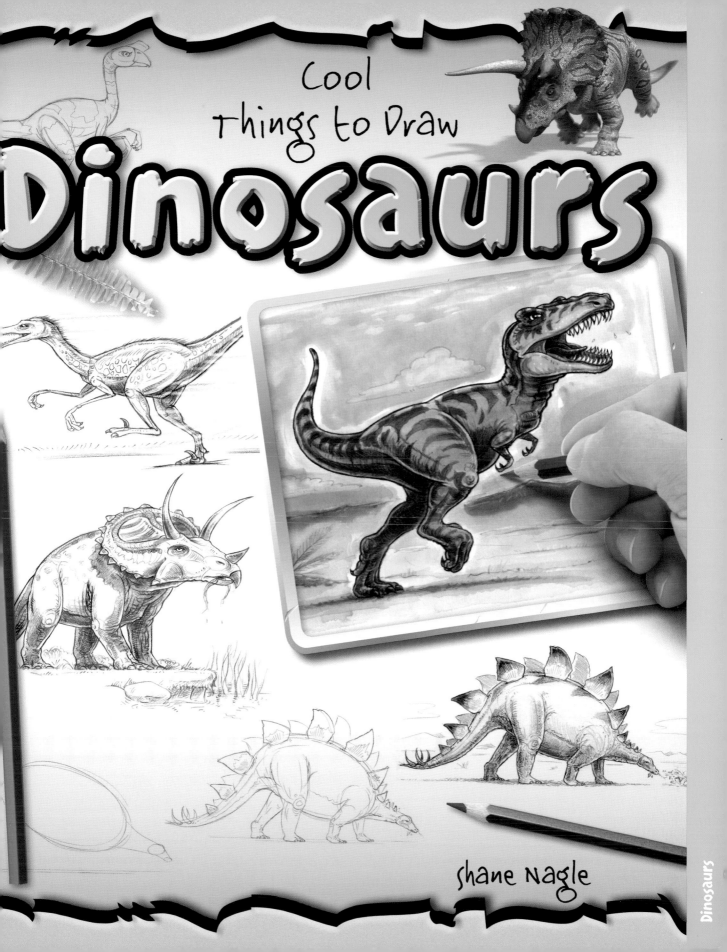

# Cool things to Draw

# Dinosaurs

Shane Nagle

# INTRODUCTION

*Dinosaurs are wonderful to draw. They have unusual shapes, with lots of teeth, claws, horns, and armor. There are many, details that are great fun to draw!*

*Before you begin, imagine you are on an archaeological dig. You have been given the task of assembling a collection of dinosaur bones and making them come to life in a drawing.*

## THINGS YOU WILL NEED

- A #2 pencil
- A clean eraser
- Sheets of paper
- A pencil sharpener
- A ruler
- A sense of humor and a positive attitude. Enjoy!

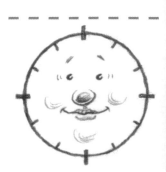

## Using the clock-face

This fun tip will help you sketch lines at different angles.
*Look at the line you want to draw.*
*Now imagine that line on a clock-face: where would it point?*
*Draw a line on your page, matching the angle on the imaginary clock-face.*

## Drawing guidelines

When drawing your dinosaurs, pay attention to these things:
1  Each drawing begins with basic shapes and simple lines
2  Always draw lightly at first
3  Focus on one part of the drawing at a time
4  Build texture and volume in layers
5  Experiment with different pencil techniques as you go
6  Practice, practice, practice!

# Step-by-step drawing

Each drawing is made by following steps. Read through all the steps carefully before you begin, then follow them one at a time until your drawing is done. Don't worry if your drawing looks different to the examples; all artists find their own style and your skills will improve with practice.

Step 1     Step 2     Step 3     Step 4

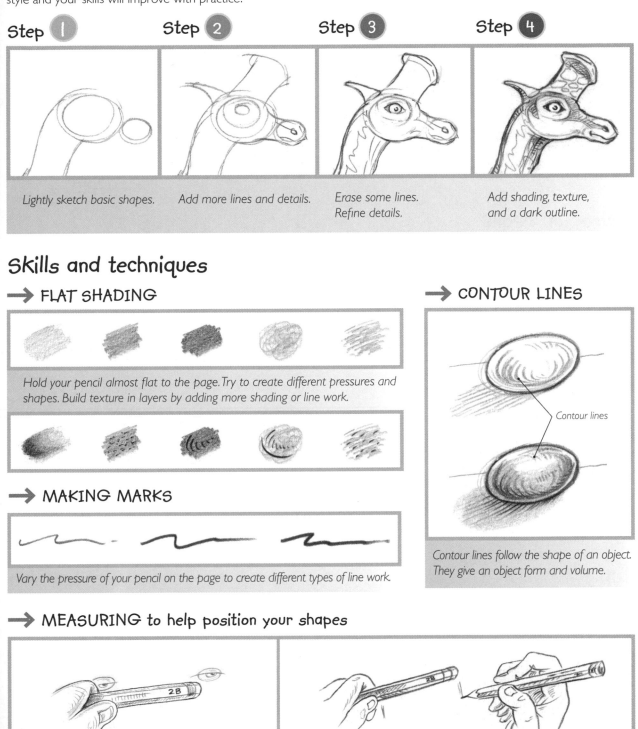

*Lightly sketch basic shapes.*    *Add more lines and details.*    *Erase some lines. Refine details.*    *Add shading, texture, and a dark outline.*

# Skills and techniques

## → FLAT SHADING

*Hold your pencil almost flat to the page. Try to create different pressures and shapes. Build texture in layers by adding more shading or line work.*

## → MAKING MARKS

*Vary the pressure of your pencil on the page to create different types of line work.*

## → CONTOUR LINES

Contour lines

*Contour lines follow the shape of an object. They give an object form and volume.*

## → MEASURING to help position your shapes

*Use a pencil like a ruler, marking the distance with your thumb. Mark that length with another pencil on your paper.*

# APATOSAURUS

*Apatosaurus was one of the largest land animals that ever existed. It had a long neck with a tiny head and brain. Its long neck allowed it to reach leaves at the top of tall trees, as well as keeping its head safe from attack by predators. The Apatosaurus had a long tail that acted as a counter-balance to its long neck.*

Meaning of name: deceptive lizard

Time period: 157–146 million years ago
Size: 68–82 feet (21–25 meters) long
Weight: 27–33 tons (25–30 tonnes)
Diet: plants

## Before you begin

Notice how an oval shape forms the main part of this drawing. The rest of it is created by building on this simple shape and adding detail.

## Step

Start with an oval shape for the body, using the clock-face to create the correct angle. Draw the baseline and add a smaller baseline for the far leg. Add a long neck to the top end of the oval, with two circles at the top for a head. Sketch the four legs with ovals at the ends for feet.

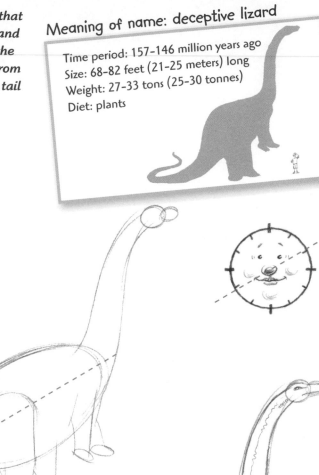

## Step

Add long narrowing lines for the tail. Create the body shape by curving the outline in and out of the original oval shape. Try to draw the line from tail to head in a single, smooth stroke. Turn the page around if it makes this easier. Define the snout and head, adding an eye, brow, and mouth. Add toes and some preliminary skin texture marks.

## Step 3

Erase any unnecessary lines and darken the rest, adding a few wrinkles on the belly and tail. Begin to give your drawing volume by using contour lines and shading, especially on the underside.

## DRAWING TIP

Give a surface texture by cross-hatching. Draw a series of short parallel lines, and add more lines next to this in an x-shaped pattern. Keep overlapping and bunching lines up to make it darker.

## Step 4

Add more texture by adding lines and cross-hatching. Shade the legs on the far side of the Apatosaurus to make them appear further away. Add a simple horizon line with some mountains. Add some shaded ground and stones under the dinosaur to give the picture perspective.

*Leave a slight gap*

INTERESTING FACT → At one stage, it was incorrectly thought that the Brontosaurus was a separate species to the Apatosaurus. However, it is now known that Brontosaurus bones were misclassified and actually belong to the Apatosaurus.

# LAMBEOSAURUS

*Lambeosaurus was the largest of the duck-billed dinosaurs. Its most obvious feature was a large crest on the top of its skull. Males had a two-pronged crest, while females had only one prong. Like many of the herbivorous dinosaurs, it lived in a herd. It's thought in Lambeosaurus' best defense from hungry carnivores was its good hearing and vision, and its ability to run very fast.*

Meaning of name: Lambe's lizard
Time period: 82–65 million years ago
Size: 49 feet (15 meters) long
Weight: 5.5 tons (5 tonnes)
Diet: plants

## Before you begin

Note the muscular legs and how much thicker and longer the back ones are compared to the front. Use two baselines in this drawing, as one of the back feet sits higher up in the picture because it is further away.

## Step 1

Draw an angled oval for the body and two smaller circles for the head. Join two s-shapes to the circles to form the neck. Add two long curved lines that meet together to create the tail. Don't forget to sketch the two baselines.

## Step 2

Sketch ovals for the ankles. Lightly sketch the feet, making the closer rear foot a bit larger than the other back foot. Add some more ovals for the eye socket and to help shape the skull. Sketch in the crest and the rest of the head's main features.

## Step

Draw a second line, close to the outline, along the neck, back, and tail for a strong backbone. Erase any unnecessary lines and begin to darken the outline. Define the toes and the webbing between them. Detail the eye with a dark outline to make it stand out and define the head.

### DRAWING TIP

Cross-hatching can be used to create shadow. You can also use small lines to create volume and shape.

## Step 4

Create your own pattern for the skin. Using the side of your pencil, add flat areas of gray. Scientists don't know what color dinosaur skin was and it is likely that the patterns and textures were never exactly the same on any two dinosaurs, so you can't make a mistake! Create shading and shadows to give the appearance that the dinosaur is walking.

*Cross-hatching*

**INTERESTING FACT** → Lambeosaurus walked and ran on two legs, but it is thought it spent most of its time on all four legs grazing for food.

# OVIRAPTOR

*Oviraptor was a small bird–like dinosaur with a very large brain. It was light, with strong legs and arms. It is thought it could run at 43 miles (70 kilometers) per hour. Its beak was short and toothless but very sharp. With its extremely powerful jaws, Oviraptor would have been able to smash open shellfish. Some scientists believe it may have had feathers.*

**Meaning of name: egg seizer or egg thief**

Time period: 88–70 million years ago
Size: 8 feet (2.5 meters) long
Weight: 66 pounds (30 kilograms)
Diet: plants and meat

## Before you begin

With only one foot on the ground, this dinosaur appears to be running. Spending time on shading this drawing will give it volume and realism.

## Step

Lightly draw an oval, checking your angles against a clock-face. Sketch another oval in the left side of the oval for a thigh and add a circle to the lower left for an ankle joint. Add a circle for the head to the top right of the oval and add shapes for the crest and beak.

## Step

Carefully draw narrow arms and feet with circles for the joints. Thin limbs make the Oviraptor look more agile. Add more detail to the beak and add an eye. Use curved lines and shapes to show how its long feet and hands are tucked under as it runs. Add a curving neck, connecting the head and body, and a long tail.

# Step ③

Erase any unnecessary lines. Define the large eye, the slightly down-turned brow, and the features on the head. Define the muscular legs, long fingers and toes, and sharp claws. Add skin folds and contour lines and sketch a light pattern over the body.

## DRAWING TIP

Sketch ellipses by first tracing your pencil around and around above the paper before lowering the tip on to the page. The ellipses will come out in nicer smooth shapes. Try it!

# Step ④

Sketch small soft lines for feathers on the neck. Use the side of your pencil almost flat on the paper to fill in any shadowed areas, the skin pattern, and the point of the beak. Add little wrinkles and dashes, dots, and contour lines to build up an interesting skin texture and to give the drawing volume. Press firmly with a sharp pencil to add a dark outline and detail to the skull. Add a shiny egg in a nest and some stones and unusual plants to the scene.

Look closely at the details of the eye

Leave a thin strip of white between the outline and the shading of the egg

INTERESTING FACT ➡ Oviraptors were omnivores, which means they ate almost anything edible, such as meat, eggs, seeds, plants, fish, and insects. This was unusual among dinosaurs.

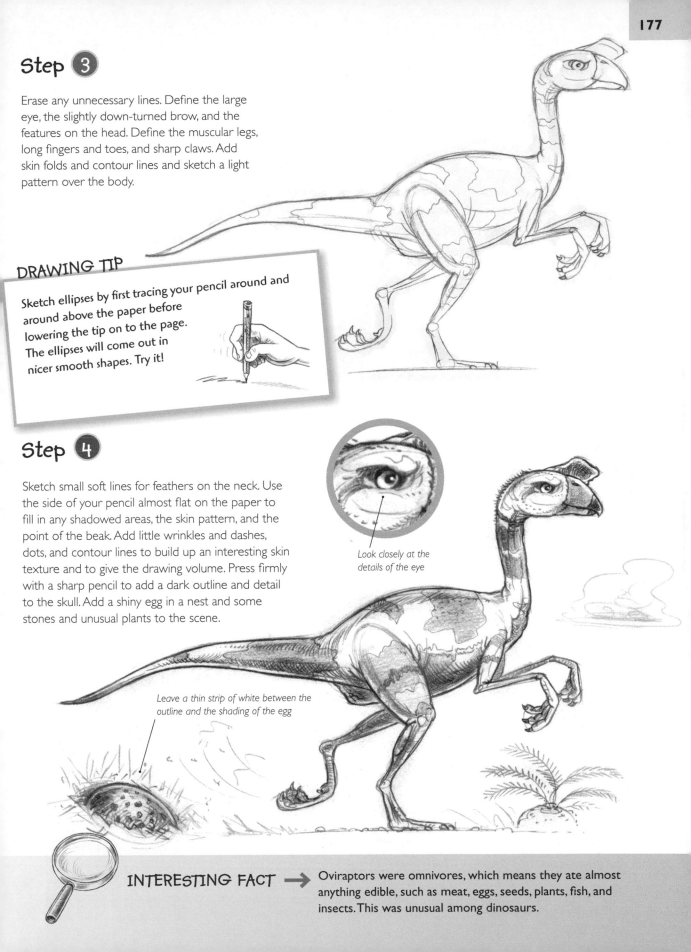

# IGUANODON

*Iguanodon's bones have been found on nearly every continent. It had a long skull, a horny toothless beak, and rows of grinding teeth. Iguanodon could run on either two or four legs and had very dextrous front feet, including long spike-like thumbs that may have been used to defend itself or to forage for food.*

Meaning of name: iguana tooth

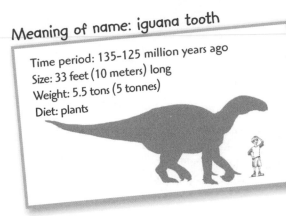

Time period: 135–125 million years ago
Size: 33 feet (10 meters) long
Weight: 5.5 tons (5 tonnes)
Diet: plants

## Before you begin

Pay attention to the unusual shape of the iguanodon's skull and the details of the feet. This drawing has some pointed areas, such as the beak. Drawing the dinosaur with two feet off the ground makes it appear to be slowly walking.

## Step 1

Sketch a large ellipse with a small oval inside. Add a circle for the head to the left above the large oval and a smaller circle for a snout next to it. Sketch a baseline below the oval.

## Step 2

Sketch small circles below the oval for the legs and feet, using your pencil and thumb to measure. Draw almost straight lines for the tail, with a slight bend towards the tip. Add lines for the neck and head, and an eye.

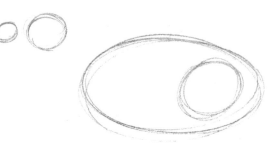

## Step ③

Sketch slightly curved lines for each section of the legs and feet. Add flat and pointed shapes for the beak, with the upper part deeper than the lower. Start to build up some details of the feet and head.

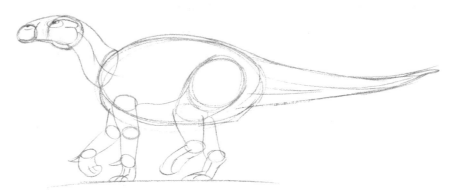

## Step ④

Erase any unnecessary lines. Define the outline with a sharp pencil. Add details as you go, such as uneven lines, wrinkles, muscles, and claws. Make the eye strong and dark. With a softer line, add skin patterns and begin to mark out body contours.

### DRAWING TIP

Give your dinosaur expression by shaping its eyes. In this example, shading under the eye, black pupils with a small highlight, and a slightly angled eyebrow give a serious and concentrated expression.

## Step ⑤

Build up the skin texture and body contours using layers. Use the side of your pencil for soft flat shading and the tip for a mixture of light and heavy line work. Use small dots and dashes to make the skin look rough. Go over some of the outlines to make them darker, especially those in shadow areas. Create a background scene with mountains and trees. Sketch grass and rocks under the dinosaur.

INTERESTING FACT ➡ Because it was so common, Iguanodon was one of the first dinosaurs ever discovered by humans.

# BRACHIOSAURUS

*Brachiosaurus was one of the largest dinosaurs that existed. It used its long neck to reach the treetops, grazing on fruit and leaves that no other creature could reach. Its front legs were much longer than its rear legs, like a giraffe's.*

## Before you begin

This drawing uses ellipses to help create the shapes of the knees and ankles. Use the side of your pencil to shade the flat gray areas.

Meaning of name: arm lizard

Time period: 161–146 million years ago
Size: 85 feet (26 meters) long and
52 feet (16 meters) tall
Weight: 53–62 tons (48–56 tonnes)
Diet: plants

## Step

Lightly sketch a large, angled ellipse and overlap it with a circle at the top. Use the clock-face to check the angles. Sketch a circle for the head at the top right and add a shape for the snout. Place an ellipse to the left of the body shapes for the curve of the tail. Add small circles under the body for the leg joints, measuring how far apart they are with your pencil and thumb. Draw a main baseline and a small baseline underneath, a fraction under the main one.

## Step

Create the body, neck, and tail using long flowing lines, curving the tail around the small ellipse. Draw the legs around the small circles, defining the toes and placing the back foot on the lower baseline. Some of the circles are smaller than the width of the legs to show the shape of the ankle, knee, or foot and to indicate that this part is a moving joint. Add an eye and some features to the head.

*Second baseline*

## Step ③

Erase any unnecessary lines. Pressing firmly with a sharp pencil, define the dinosaur's outline, adding wrinkles and folds in the skin. Draw a mouth, keeping it straight and level. Give your drawing volume by using contour lines for muscles on the legs, neck, and tail. These will help when shading.

### DRAWING TIP

To create flat shadow areas, hold your pencil on its side, almost flat to the paper, and gently move it in circles or in a back-and-forth motion.

## Step ④

Add more wrinkles and lines using soft and hard pencil work. Build up the detail in layers. Using the side of a pencil, create a soft flat shadow on the two middle legs. Add shadows under the tail, on the neck, and on the ground. Go over some of the outlines with a darker line, especially those in the shadow areas. Using soft lines, draw an erupting volcano, some smoke clouds, and a simple landscape.

**INTERESTING FACT** → Brachiosaurus would have needed a very strong, muscular heart to pump blood up its long neck to its head and brain and around its massive body.

# ELASMOSAURUS

*Elasmosaurus has been described as a "snake threaded through the body of a turtle." Its neck was up to 20 feet (6 meters) long; nearly half its entire length. It used its four paddle-like flippers to swim. Elasmosaurus is not technically a dinosaur: it is a plesiosaur, meaning "close to a lizard." Most marine dinosaurs were actually plesiosaurs.*

**Meaning of name: thin-plated lizard**

Time period: 65 million years ago
Size: 45 feet (14 meters) long
Weight: 2 tons (2 tonnes)
Diet: fish

## Before you begin

This drawing is made of simple shapes and uses lots of lines and shading to suggest volume, especially on the body. Use swirling soft lines to create water ripples and an eraser to create sunlight highlights.

## Step

Sketch a large, angled ellipse for the body. To the lower left, draw a circle to indicate the curve of the long, snake-like neck. Add a circle below the body for the head and a small circle inside it for an eye. To create the snout, draw an oblique rectangle (a rectangle where the corners are not at right angles).

## Step 2

Draw curved rectangles for the flippers, attaching them to the body shape. Sketch the neck around the circle, narrowing it as it gets closer to the head. Add a pointed tail.

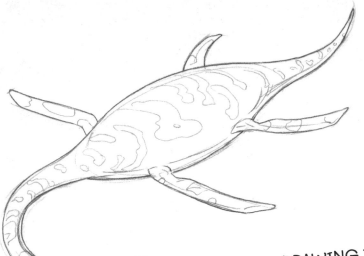

## Step 3

Erase any unnecessary lines. Press firmly with a sharp pencil to define the long smooth neck and the body, flipper, and tail shapes. Add details to the snake-like head. Create soft patterns for the skin texture, remembering to follow the rounded contours of the body parts.

### DRAWING TIP

Use a dirty eraser to smudge gray areas and a clean eraser to add highlights by removing parts of the drawing. This creates an underwater effect.

## Step 4

Build up the contours of the body in layers. Use the side of your pencil to create soft shadow areas. Fill in some of the skin pattern, pressing harder in darker areas and gradually lightening the pencil pressure as you move into brighter areas. Leave a thin gap between outlines and nearby shadows or contours to show where the sun is reflected. Use your eraser to remove parts of the drawing so the creature looks like it is underwater. Add soft lines for ripples, bubbles, and a few tube-like fish.

INTERESTING FACT → Elasmosaurus fossils have been found with small stones in the stomach. It is thought these were used to help digest food.

# STEGOSAURUS

*The armored back and tail of Stegosaurus make it one of the most distinctive and well-recognized dinosaurs. Some of its arrowhead-shaped plates were over 30 inches (75 centimeters) long. With rear legs twice as long as its front legs, Stegosaurus's head was near to the ground. It could swing its spiked tail to inflict serious injury if attacked.*

Meaning of name: roof lizard

Time period: 156–140 million years ago
Size: 30 feet (9 meters) long
Weight: 3.3 tons (3 tonnes)
Diet: plants

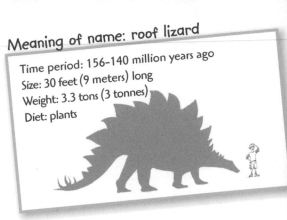

## Before you begin

Pay attention to the highlighted areas with less gray along the outer edge of the armor plates. The plates are shaded from a soft gray to almost black, with rough edges as though this creature has seen a few fights. The Stegosaurus in this drawing has lots of wrinkles over its body.

## Step 1

Create a large, angled ellipse, drawing lightly and fast. Sketch two parallel baselines close to each other, both slanting downhill very slightly. Add a circle to the lower side of the oval for the head and shapes for the snout. Draw the neck, connecting the head to the body. Add a tail.

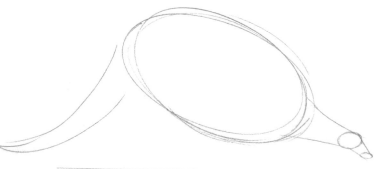

## Step 2

Draw two circles for the top of the legs. Sketch the legs, making the rear ones thicker and longer than the front legs. Add two feet on the near side of the body on the lower baseline and two on the far side on the upper baseline. Two feet are flat on the ground and two have their ankles raised. Draw circles for the leg joints and add some facial features. Sketch the armor plates, starting at the back leg and leaving space between each triangular shape.

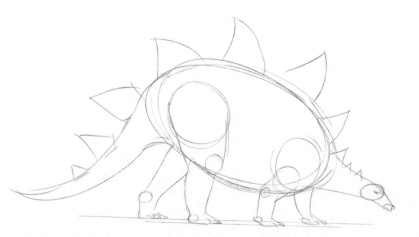

# Step ③

Erase any unnecessary lines. Add wrinkles and details to the head and skin. Softly and roughly sketch more triangles between the first ones, angling them slightly toward the back.
With a sharp pencil, give the first plates a strong shape, making each one unique. Add toes and the four horns on the tail.

*Leaving white space around an object makes it appear to be closer*

## DRAWING TIP

The softly drawn ripples around the bottom of each plate make the armor appear to be growing through the skin. Leaving white space around an object makes it appear closer. More lightly drawn objects appear further away.

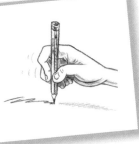

*Ripples in skin make the armor appear to be stuck into it*

# Step ④

Build the shadow areas and texture in layers. Change the pressure and the angle of your pencil work as you shade, sometimes using a sharp pencil and sometimes a blunter one. This adds variety and interest to your drawing. Add mountains in the background and some plants for the Stegosaurus to eat. Add some cross-hatched shadows under the body.

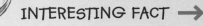

## INTERESTING FACT →

It is thought that the plates along Stegosaurus's back were used to control its body temperature. They may also have been used for defense or as a display to either attract a mate or scare away predators.

# VELOCIRAPTOR

One of the most intelligent dinosaurs on the planet, Velociraptor was capable of running 37 miles (60 kilometers) an hour, making it one of the fastest land animals. It is thought this light and agile hunter ate just about any meat it could find, including many plant eaters. A fossil has been discovered of a Velociraptor locked in battle with a Protoceratops twenty times its own weight.

## Before you begin

The Velociraptor is drawn with most of its body weight leaning forward so that it appears to be running swiftly. Add action and speed to your drawing by using an eraser and the side of a pencil to add movement lines.

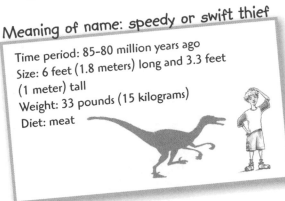

Meaning of name: speedy or swift thief

Time period: 85–80 million years ago
Size: 6 feet (1.8 meters) long and 3.3 feet (1 meter) tall
Weight: 33 pounds (15 kilograms)
Diet: meat

## Step 1

Drawing lightly, sketch a thin, angled ellipse, using the clock-face as a guide. Add a smaller ellipse inside the first one, on a sharper angle. Add an ellipse for the head to the top right and sketch lines to show the snout. Add a baseline underneath the ellipses and another line near the head to use as a guide for the length of the snout.

## Step 2

Draw a tail, using your pencil to measure the length. Ensure the bottom tail line connects smoothly to the bottom of the main ellipse. Add a few small circles to mark the leg joints and shoulder, two s-shaped lines for the neck, and some eye and jaw details. Sketch the leg and arm shapes.

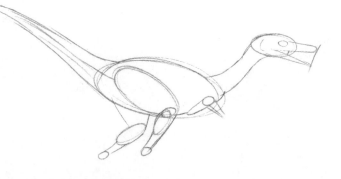

## Step 3

Use your eraser to remove any unnecessary lines. Add more details, focusing on the head and feet. Draw the raised rear foot parallel to the ground. Use pointy shapes for claws and lots of dashes for teeth.

## Step 4

Erase any more unnecessary lines, then sharpen your pencil and build the outline. Add feathery lines down the neck, back, and tail. Add the outlines of the toes and claws, and define the eye so it has a wild look. Sketch some contour lines, wrinkles, folds, and texture.

## DRAWING TIP

Give eyes a wild look. Use a mirror to see how your eyes look with a variety of facial expressions, and then practice them in your drawings.

## Step 5

Build up the skin texture and body contours with layers of shading and line work. Use the side of your pencil for soft flat shading and the tip of the pencil for a mixture of light and heavy line work. Use little dots and dashes to make the skin look rough. Go over some of the outlines to darken them, especially those in shadow areas.

INTERESTING FACT → The Velociraptor had a retractable, 3.5 inch (9 centimeter) long, sickle-shaped claw on each foot that swiveled downward when it was ready to attack.

# TRICERATOPS

*Triceratops was heavier than an African bull elephant and resembles a modern-day rhinoceros. Its 10 foot (3 meter) long skull was the largest of any land animal. It is thought Triceratops moved in herds, hatched from eggs, and fought in mating rituals. It had a tough beak like a parrot's and the shield on its head was made of bone.*

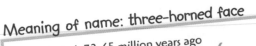

Meaning of name: three-horned face

Time period: 72–65 million years ago
Size: 30 feet (9 meters) long
Weight: 11 tons (10 tonnes)
Diet: plants

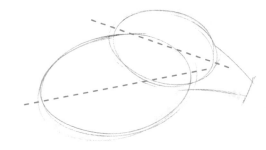

## Before you begin

This Triceratops is drawn as if it is being looked at from ground level. The skull shield is tilted back and away to emphasize the horns. Build lots of shadow and texture in layers under the belly and on the skull shield.

## Step

Draw lightly at first. Using the clock-face, draw two angled ellipses crossing over each other at one end. Use your thumb or a pencil to measure the spacing. Sketch a baseline under the ellipses and add lines for the snout.

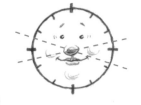

## Step

Sketch a tail almost touching the ground. Add two ellipses for the upper legs, and then finish the rest of the legs and the feet, adding circles for the rear leg joints. Draw ellipses for the eye and an ellipse for the base of the biggest horn. Sketch in the rest of the horns.

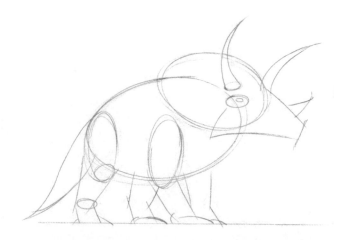

# Step 3

Erase any unnecessary lines. Lightly sketch the grassy ground and the riverbank. Add details to the skin and feet, and build the small triangles around the rim of shield, the shapes on the shield, and the circles on the head (this is the most challenging part of this drawing). Define the eye and add some grass in the mouth.

# Step 4

Erase any unnecessary lines. Define the outline with a sharp pencil. With a lighter touch, add curves on the shield and horns, and give volume to the belly and legs using contour lines. Add a heavy, dark line to the eye and add a pupil. Create soft gray shading above the eye, so it seems to be shadowed by the outer brow. Shade heavily inside the mouth and nostril.

## DRAWING TIP

Create great looking horns using a combination of:
(i) contour lines (curves)
(ii) shading (soft and dark)
and
(iii) highlights

# Step 5

Use lots of variety to create texture, building it in layers. Start with your pencil almost flat (on its side), shading the larger areas in a flat gray. Use darker shading under the skull and belly, leaving a gap along each edge as a highlight. Add squiggly lines, dots, and dashes to decorate the skin. Add more detail to the grass and river, and a few drops of water falling from the grass in the mouth.

 **INTERESTING FACT** → Scientists are unsure whether the Triceratops used its horns and shield for defense, like a charging rhinoceros, or for courtship and display, like a reindeer.

# TYRANNOSAURUS REX

*Tyrannosaurus rex was one of the most fearsome predators to have existed. With up to fifty serrated-edged teeth locked inside a massive and powerful jaw, Tyrannosaurus rex could easily crush bones and rip through the toughest flesh. It took giant, 16 foot (5 meter) long steps when running. Its arms were tiny but extremely strong, possibly so it could hold struggling prey as it attacked.*

Meaning of name: tyrant lizard king

Time period: 80–65 million years ago
Size: 46 feet (14 meters) long and 20 feet (6 meters) high
Weight: 7.7 tons (7 tonnes)
Diet: meat

## Before you begin

The head is drawn so you can see inside the mouth, with its large, curved sharp teeth. The guidelines for the jaws are not straight or square, and the lower one cuts through the bottom of the head circle.

## Step

Pressing lightly with your pencil, sketch an angled ellipse. Use the clock-face to create the correct angle. Add a circle for the head and guidelines for the jaws. Draw a baseline under the ellipse and a pointed tail. Sketch circles for the leg joints.

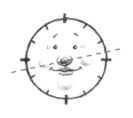

## Step

Sketch an ellipse for the near thigh and add the rest of the leg. Draw the back leg and foot, using curved instead of straight lines. Shape the head, adding wavy lines for the jaw. Create the details of the eye, brow, and nose. Add extra lines for the neck and back.

## Step ③

Use your eraser to erase any unnecessary lines. Don't worry if you rub out too much, as you can always sketch it again. Go over the outline with a heavier pencil, defining the head, jaw, feet, and claws. Add wrinkles and folds to the body and a tongue in the mouth. Sharpen your pencil before you sketch in the teeth.

### DRAWING TIP

To prevent smudging your drawing, turn your page around or stand up and draw.

## Step ④

Erase any unnecessary lines and define the outlines. Build up the shapes and volume of each body part in layers, using the side of your pencil and contour lines. Add shading, wrinkles, folds, and texture to the skin and darken the area inside the mouth and tongue, and around the eyes. Use cross-hatching to shade the shadowed areas. Sketch a simple landscape in the background. Add some movement lines around the legs and the tail and a few drops of saliva around the mouth.

INTERESTING FACT ➔ When one of its 6 inch (15 centimeter) long teeth broke or became worn, Tyrannosaurus rex would simply grow another one.

**hinkler**

Published by Hinkler Books Pty Ltd 2012
45–55 Fairchild Street
Heatherton Victoria 3202 Australia
www.hinkler.com.au

© Hinkler Books Pty Ltd 2008, 2012

Text and Illustrations: Shane Nagle
Internal Design: Aspace Studio
Editors: Hinkler Design Studio and Simone Egger
Cover Design: Hinkler Design Studio
Prepress: Graphic Print Group

ISBN 978 1 7430 8891 3

Printed and bound in China